Hearing God's Heart Beat

Developing Greater Intimacy with God in the Midst of Intense Battles

DeAnna Kitchens

Hearing God's Heart Beat
by DeAnna Kitchens

Printed in the United States of America

ISBN 9781615798384

www.xulonpress.com

Table of Contents

Hearing God's Heart Beat: *Developing Greater Intimacy with God in the Midst of Intense Battles*

Introduction

Have you ever lain next to someone so close you could hear his heart beat? Hear the thumping, pulsing sound. Feel the pounding. It almost seems like your body beats with the same rhythm.

Two people

Hearts beating

Perfectly in step

Have you ever been so close to God you hear his heart beat? Have you heard the rhythm? The thumping? Felt the pounding? That's how close God wants us to be to him.

His desires become my desires.

His plans become my plans.

His passion becomes my passion.

His heartbeat becomes my heartbeat.

Through a series of frustrations, disappointments and seemingly impossible battles, I began a journey of purposefully listening for God's heartbeat. I want to hear his heart beat; to know he's that close. My heart truly desires more of God. Not just for clock time, but a deep intimate relationship.

My life, probably no different than yours, has had flashes of extreme exhilaration and instances of agonizing pain. Although the pain may seem at the time to last forever, in the whole scheme of things, it is an instance or a flash of time.

In the following pages, I'm sharing with you my journey to hear God's heart beat even in the midst of excruciating physical, emotional, and relational pain. I have learned how being close to God can help you survive anything. I encourage you, as you read, to allow God to show you who He is and how much He desires intimacy with you.

Chapter 1 – Pain is Such a Lonely Place

Psalm 18:6 But in my distress I cried out to the LORD; yes, I prayed to my God for help. He heard me from his sanctuary; my cry reached his ears.

Pain is a "state of physical, emotional, or mental lack of well-being or physical, emotional, or mental uneasiness ranging from mild discomfort or dull distress to acute often unbearable agony." Pain may be generalized or localized, and is the consequence of being injured or hurt physically or mentally or of some derangement of or lack of equilibrium in the physical or mental functions (as through disease), and that usually produces a reaction of wanting to avoid, escape, or destroy the causative factor and its effects pain.[i]

At some point in each of our lives we will or already have dealt with pain. Pain comes in so many different forms – cuts and scrapes, emotional suffering, severe physical pain, spiritual drought, mental torment, and so on. Sometimes pain lasts for a brief moment and others a lifetime. There seems to be no rhyme or reason for who experiences what kind of pain or how much of it. We can't map it out. And really, only those who have experienced deep pain can understand it.

As I write, I can tell you that I have experienced deep ongoing pain for a long time and it has been a very desolate place. However, God is always faithful and is enough no matter what we feel. There are days when I know the only way I can move is if God miraculously moves me.

~ Physical Pain ~

I began to experience physical pain with migraine headaches almost every day when I was in junior high. Imagine someone stabbing an ice pick in the side of your head over and over again, plus a little nausea for good measure. Sometimes the headaches would last a few hours, sometimes they would last for weeks at a time. I didn't realize they were migraines until years later. I was told by doctors that I was too young to have headaches and by others that it was in my head. Well, yeah, it was in my head. It was my head that was hurting! Unfortunately, I did not grow out of the headaches. I still have them regularly. My late twenties and early thirties were the worst years for the migraines. I think my work schedule and daily stress impacted the frequency and intensity of the headaches. There were a number of days I worked in my office with the lights off to try to reduce the piercing pain. Because I have had the headaches for so many years, I can almost always just block the pain now. I've learned to ignore the pounding, stabbing pain so I am able to function.

When I turned twenty, it seemed like my body started falling apart. On top of the almost daily migraines, I developed endometriosis. Endometriosis is a condition where tissue lesions form in the lower abdomen and pelvic area. The primary symptom is pelvic pain and many women with endometriosis cannot have children. I remember walking in the mall on a Saturday afternoon with my husband, Jimmy, and my parents. Just a short time after we arrived, I was doubled over in gut-wrenching pain from the endometriosis. After two surgeries in six months and a six-month long chemical treatment for the endometriosis, I was temporarily relieved of the endometriosis pain. Then, I got pregnant.

During my pregnancy, I was sick from the first week to the last day. I was hospitalized three times and was so sick I almost died. I worked 50-60 hours a week and went to the doctor at lunch some days to be given an IV to combat the dehydration. I was so sick the third time I was in the hospital, I barely remember it. I know I was really sick but I faded in and out so much the whole experience is a blur. During this particular hospital visit, I was fed lipids through an IV for a week. We did not know it at the time but found out later the doctors were struggling to save me. By the time my precious son Taylor was born, I felt like I had been trampled on by a herd of angry elephants! There were many days I prayed to die because I just did not feel like I could handle life anymore.

When Taylor was two, we moved to Kansas. My career was really taking off and life seemed to be going well. Although I still had frequent headaches and abdominal pain, I really felt pretty good and was enjoying my work. Then, I started having the intense endometriosis pain again and a constant tiredness that never seemed to go away. After a visit with my gynecologist, we decided I needed a hysterectomy because of the return of the endometriosis pain. So, he did the surgery and discovered I actually had a cancerous tumor. In a way, having the endometriosis saved my life. The doctors had no clue I had cancer and it was really a miracle he even saw it. The tumor was removed during the surgery and I've been cancer free since then.

After the surgery, my career continued to grow. I finished my master's degree and became a management/human resource consultant and trainer. Business was going great and I was very successful in my work. I was good at what

I did and I loved my job. I would go in to a business, help them identify problems, recommend solutions and then, implement solutions to make them more successful.

We were able to buy our first house after eleven years of marriage. Life was good, but I still had an everyday pain and fatigue I couldn't figure out. I wasn't sure what was causing it, all I knew was I didn't feel good.

Then around my thirtieth birthday, the pain went to a whole new level. My previous experiences with pain and sickness actually prepared me for the new pain. If I had never experienced pain before, I don't know how I would have managed the new pain. This pain was different than anything I had experienced. Every joint in my body hurts. Every movement causes pain. Picture your joints being glass with raw nerves surrounding them. Then, clamp on the nerve-covered glass a massive vice grip. As you try to move, the vice grip tightens and the glass feels like it is on the verge of shattering. Stiff, painful, and swollen, I could barely stand up without help. My muscles ache like I've overused them all day every day. I went to several doctors, chiropractors, and tried a variety of natural treatments. I loved the massage therapy; unfortunately it didn't fix my pain. None of the doctors knew what was wrong and nothing they did helped. I was told it's fibromyalgia by some and then others said fibromyalgia is just made up and it's really just stress.

I think not knowing what's wrong is worse than knowing and it being something bad. When you don't know, your mind thinks of all the varying possibilities – none of them good – and then you start to feel like you're just crazy. I can't tell you how many times I had doctors tell me it was all in my head. That was frustrating, infuriating and depressing. I actually started to question myself – am I imagining this? But, I knew the pain was real.

My first glimpse of hope in identifying my ailment was from a chiropractor. What he said was shocking (coming from a chiropractor ☺). He told me he couldn't help me and I didn't need to come back to see him. He said the symptoms and his exam indicate I had rheumatoid arthritis (RA) and there was nothing he could do to help me. This realization was scary and good at the same time. I felt like I had something to pursue, yet I was afraid of what the diagnosis might mean.

The more research I did about the disease, the more I was afraid. There is no cure for RA. It is an auto-immune disease where basically your body attacks itself. With RA, you ultimately end up with deformed joints and potentially complete disability.

We had recently moved and found new doctors. Our new family doctor was an absolute godsend. After actually talking to me, listening to what I had to say, and examining me, he concurred rheumatoid arthritis was very likely. He referred me to a rheumatologist, who has been remarkable. She, too, listened and asked questions and thoughtfully examined and began diagnosing. She determined I have rheumatoid arthritis and fibromyalgia. This determination was made in 2003.

As the months came and went, my pain and fatigue steadily increased. Many days I cannot stand up without help. When you have chronic pain, the doctors ask you to rate your pain on a ten-point scale, with one being practically no pain and ten being the most severe just-shoot-me-and-get-it-over-with pain. My pain level is almost always seven or higher. In addition to excruciating pain in my joints, I am constantly exhausted. There's a cycle that takes place – pain causes sleeping difficulties that result in exhaustion and increased pain causing less sleep. I've lived this debilitating cycle for more than fifteen years. As the RA has progressed, I am becoming severely limited in what I can do. I am a very independent person. Depending on other people for things I should do is frustrating. I can no longer shop for groceries by myself. Taylor is my grocery shopping buddy. He pushes the cart, let's me hold on to him as we walk, picks up the items and places them in the cart and loads and unloads the groceries. He has been such a huge blessing. On Sundays, I get up, get dressed, go to church, eat lunch, and crash for the rest of the day. By the time I get home from church, my pain is at a level nine. Everything I do comes at a price.

The treatments for the RA frequently made me sick. We tried a whole host of medications, ranging from chemo medications to biologic IV infusions. While the medications have protected my joints from deformity, they have not removed the pain, stiffness or fatigue that plagues me every day.

With medications not taking away the pain, stiffness, swelling, and fatigue, I began to wonder if we were missing something. Was there something else wrong with me? Were we on the totally wrong course? Were there other medications we could try? So, with much influence from everyone around me, I decided to get a second opinion. I drove myself three and a half hours away to Kansas City to see the doctor. I allowed myself to have hope this doctor would see something or have some kind of answer for why I wasn't getting better. He did a lot of lab work and then, spent about 10 minutes with me. I wanted him to ask questions, exam me and use diagnostic skills. Instead, he looked at my history and said yep, you have RA and that was it. He didn't critically think about anything or look for alternatives or missed diagnosis. He just concurred. I was totally devastated when I left. All I could think was it's not going to get better, there is no hope. I was so angry and upset. As I headed home, I was bawling and driving. Honestly, I don't think I even paid attention to where I was going. I stopped in a shopping center parking lot, parked the car and cried. At that point, I felt utterly hopeless, like life will never get better.

I have always believed I could do anything, survive anything and nothing was going to stop me. For the three years of seeking a diagnosis and the first year after the diagnosis, no one even knew except my parents & Jimmy. Not a soul. The second year, I told a couple of friends. That was it. No one knew and no one had any idea. I was good, really good, at hiding the pain when I was around people. Then I would completely crash when I was at home. I felt like if I told people then, I wouldn't be 'tough' anymore. It would be like I was giving up, giving in to the disease. Probably one of the hardest things for me to do was begin to tell people what was wrong with me. It felt like admitting I had RA to people was letting the RA win. Sounds silly, huh?

I remember one of my consulting engagements involved facilitating management training. Each training session was about six hours and I had four sessions. By the end of the first day, my feet were so swollen my shoes cut into the skin and my feet were bleeding. After the clients left the room, my brave happy face quickly disappeared as I couldn't even take a step without searing pain in my feet, knees, and hips. I couldn't lift my arms up to pull the flip chart off the easel. I knew I had to pack all my training supplies and materials, load the car, and then, drive four hours to get home. I wasn't even sure I could get to the door of the room, much less the car. So, I did the only thing I knew to do. I prayed. While God didn't remove the pain, He did help me have the strength to load the car and get home alive. Similar scenes have been repeated day after day.

> *Psalm 18:6 But in my distress I cried out to the LORD; yes, I prayed to my God for help. He heard me from his sanctuary; my cry reached his ears.*

I'm a dreamer, strategizer, big picture, set a goal and achieve it person. I'm driven to succeed. I'm passionate about helping people. But here I was; I couldn't even stand up for ten minutes without feeling like I was going to crumble.

At this same time, God had given me and my husband, Jimmy, a dream to create a missions organization. We were beyond enthusiastic about what God was calling us to do. We had no idea how hard it would be and what a long process it would be. We had a dream bigger than life, a fantastic career, and a disease totally knocking me flat on the floor.

Physical pain is a lonely place.

~ Emotional & Mental Pain ~

Emotional and mental pain comes in a variety of ways: fear, shame, guilt, lack of self-worth, hopelessness, grief, unhappiness, assault, loss and more. It can be inflicted upon us by someone else, by a specific set of circumstances, by our own actions or reactions, or by physiological conditions. I've worked with a lot of people in my career and as a minister's wife, I've watched as individuals feel trapped, crushed, and incapacitated by emotional and mental pain.

When I was in third grade, my family moved to an area in south Dallas. My dad was the new pastor at the church in town. Looking back on my life, this was a pivotal point for me. In fact, the three years there shaped how I responded to life for many years to come. Being the new kid in school was not new to me but it didn't make it any easier. You walk through the door and a target magically appears on your forehead. Everyone looks at you, talks about you and in my case makes fun of you. I was called names because I was the only white kid in many of the classes. It was miserable! In the fourth grade, my English teacher asked me to give the spelling tests to my class because she couldn't pronounce all the words. Again, I became another big target. No one likes the teacher's pet. I wish I would have known the consequences of being the teacher's pet then. During those school years, I had bullies make fun of me, laugh at me, write threatening notes, and I was scared every day. I would go to the bathroom and be swarmed by the bullies looking under the door and climbing up to look over the stall as they made fun of me.

At the same time all of this was happening, my family had several creepy things occur at home. First, someone put sugar in the gas tank of our car. Then, someone poisoned our dog, Corky. So, we had to have Corky put to sleep. When my sister and I would get home from school, we started getting hang-up calls and some threatening phone calls. Finally, when we moved, someone cut the break lines on our moving truck. My dad was driving the truck and my sister and I were sitting between him and mom. All the sudden, dad was trying to stop the truck and it wouldn't stop. He engaged the emergency brake and we finally came to a stop. The mechanic said the brake line had obviously been cut.

With all of these events, I became very fearful and withdrawn. I didn't realize the profound effect these years had on me until I was almost thirty. Throughout junior high and high school I had a very difficult time making friends. I was extremely self-conscious. I tried to disappear, where no one would even notice I was in the room. I didn't want to be noticed. I skipped lunch almost every day because I didn't know where to sit in the lunchroom. The few days I went through the line and got food, I walked into the sitting area, looked around, threw my food away and walked out. I was so scared of people I didn't know how to talk to anyone.

It took me a long time to identify and deal with the emotional scars resulting in the fear, lack of confidence and isolation. Emotional and mental pain may be easy to identify but is frequently challenging to conquer.

Most of us can relate to stress on some level. Have you ever been in survival mode? You know, the place where you aren't really making progress in anything, just trying to survive without getting buried alive. There are times when I feel trapped in survival mode. It's not a fun place and it is certainly not productive or healthy. If you stay in survival mode too long, the emotional and mental stress can actually have physical consequences, such as heart problems, headaches, muscle tension and many more. Our bodies respond to stress with increased heart rate, faster more shallow breathing and contraction of our muscles. The physical response to stress is a warning sign or a self-protection mechanism designed by our Creator to prevent long-term damage to our bodies.

Jimmy, Taylor and I have constantly lived in survival mode for the last two years. I went to the grocery store last summer and spent what money we had to buy a few groceries. As I put the bags in the car, I stood there and looked at it and thought about how our whole cash value is now sitting in 8 bags in the back of our car. A few months later, we had $5 in the bank, no food in the pantry, 8 eggs and some cheese. It felt like everything God had given us over the previous years was crumbling away, slipping through our fingers. We were in jeopardy of losing everything, including our home, and nothing we did seemed to make a difference. Although we trust God and know He has a plan for us, we still felt a tremendous amount of pressure. When you can't even provide food for your family, you experience emotional and mental pain. But God always provided just enough for the moment we were in and many times the provision came from sources we never would have expected. People brought groceries to our house unsolicited. Others sent us gift cards to buy groceries. We didn't ask people for food but God used people to provide for us. Around Christmas-time, Taylor got a job for a friend decorating the restaurant where she works. He had a great time and enjoyed earning some money. Taylor brought home a turkey from our friend. We had nothing to eat in the house and had planned to have peanut butter and jelly for Christmas dinner. The next day, another friend brought a ham, potatoes, milk, and many other grocery items. We did not expect anything or even ask for anything but God knew our need and provided.

Fear is a powerful emotional pain. It plagued me for years and eroded my confidence and self-value. I still have to maintain a keen awareness of my thoughts to avoid falling into a fear trap. The journey to break free of the fear and emotional pain that gripped me took years. Stress wears us down mentally, emotionally and ultimately can impact our physical health and relationships.

Emotional and mental pain is a lonely place.

~ Relationship Pain ~

Have you ever been hurt by someone so deeply you couldn't breathe? I have and physical pain is nothing compared to the agony of pain caused by someone you love. It leaves you feeling stripped, vulnerable, violated, betrayed and in utter despair. It is hard to even find words to describe the intensity. One of the risks of having relationships is that the other person will break your heart. I can't even tell you how many times my heart has been crushed. There are a couple of times, though, I wasn't sure I would ever recover from.

Because of my childhood experiences (way more than what I have shared), I almost expected people to inflict pain. My trust level was about zero, especially for church people. I never expected a pastor to hurt us. Jimmy and I were youth pastors for seven years before we became lead pastors. We moved to a small town in Louisiana to be full-time youth pastors. This was our first full-time position. The youth group was growing and the kid's lives were being impacted in great ways. We were becoming good friends with the pastor and his wife. While the pastor's family went on vacation, Jimmy and I took care of the church services and the people. We had amazing response to Jimmy's preaching and the worship. In fact, we had a lot of positive feedback and we thought we did a great job. Well, not long after the pastor returned, he called Jimmy into the office after church on a Wednesday night and told him to write a resignation letter and turn in our keys right then. I wasn't allowed in the office while they were talking. So, I had no idea what was happening. When Jimmy walked out of the office, I saw the numb look on his face and I just cried when he told me. No warning. No explanation. No chance to say good-bye to anyone. We had to be out of town before Sunday. We felt betrayed. We were absolutely crushed by someone we thought was our friend. The relationship pain we experienced devastated us.

One of my closest friends and I were so much alike we were almost always thinking the same thing. We could finish each other's thoughts. We liked the same things. We had way too much fun together. We shared our lives with each other. We could talk about every joy and every pain we experienced. She was my closest friend other than Jimmy. Then, it seemed like almost overnight she was gone. My attempts to contact her got lost in space. I would call and email and get nothing in return. I told myself she's just busy. Every day I hoped to hear from her. I analyzed every conversation and interaction to try to figure out what I did wrong. Heartbroken doesn't adequately describe how I felt. I had a huge gaping hole in my heart and I didn't know why. After a few months we saw each other again and everything seemed normal. We had a great time, talked and laughed. Then, my calls and emails were ignored again. I lost all contact with her. During this time, I felt abandoned. When I really needed a friend, she wasn't there. She was my person. I missed her immensely. It seemed like she just totally evaporated and I was left all alone. The pain was agonizing. It sucked the life out of me. When my career was successful, I didn't have my person to celebrate with me. When Clear Vision Ministries had amazing results from our projects, I didn't have my person to rejoice with me. When I had an intensely dark time with my RA, I didn't have my person to hold my hand and pray with me. I felt so alone and abandoned. I could hardly breathe – my heart literally hurt. Yes, I had other friends but not my person.

It's interesting to me even though I know how unbearably bad my physical pain has been, remembering past physical pain doesn't affect me in any way. It's just an acknowledgement of what was. Relationship pain is another story. Even though I have completely forgiven and moved on, as I remember the events surrounding the big relationship pains, my heart skips a beat and I feel the tears wanting to pour out. It is all too easy to insulate ourselves and avoid close relationships after we have been hurt. But, God didn't make us to be alone.

Relationship pain is a lonely place.

~ Surviving the Loneliness ~

Be authentic. Take the mask off – really off. If you are truly honest, you can acknowledge that either right now or sometime in your past you have had some kind of pain. It may be physical, relational, financial, spiritual or some combination. No one is forever immune. For some of us life has been a continual series of pains appearing to incrementally increase in intensity. The more intense the pain, the lonelier it gets.

There are times when friends and family do not understand your specific situation. Some of your friends will sympathize and show compassion but sometimes you need someone who can empathize and identify with what you are experiencing. In my life, I have friends who feel bad for me and are compassionate but they do not understand the physical pain I live with everyday. Unless you have experienced chronic pain and never-ending exhaustion, it is impossible to understand. It's not the same as a headache or a pulled muscle or a twisted ankle. It's not the same as staying up too late one night or working overtime for four days in a row. It's just not the same. Even the best intentioned friends and family can say and do the most upsetting things. The comment I just love the most is, "well, you look fine so you can't be feeling too bad." The last time I heard those words, I sat in the floor in my bedroom and cried until I didn't have the strength to cry any more. My thoughts ranged from 'you don't understand the feeling of a sledgehammer banging on your shoulders' to 'I'm doing my best to smile and not fall over' to 'do you think I'm crazy.' Most of the times, I just smile and say thank you. There was a time when I tried to explain how I really felt but most of the time I looked into blank, incomprehensive eyes. It is a terribly lonely feeling when you can't think of anyone who understands what you're experiencing. Even Jimmy can't understand and he's with me all the time. He sees it but he doesn't feel it. There are days the battle seems futile and I crave having someone who understands and can tell me it will be ok. Most of the time, there is not a human around who understands but God is there and He has held my hand over and over again.

I'm blessed because I have a couple of friends who truly understand the space I'm in with my health. We can talk and understand each other, pray with each other and vent without feeling completely and utterly misunderstood. I can say it hurts to even breathe and they know exactly what I mean. We hurt for each other. I hate the fact that I have friends who are hurting and I would give anything to take their pain away. Maybe you are facing a health crisis and need someone who understands. If you do not have a friend who's been there, I highly recommend finding a support group of some kind.

For me, even more than my health, there are very few people who really understand our ministry – the intricate details of what we do, why we do it, and the sacrificial pain we have endured. I've had so many family and friends who just don't get it. They don't understand why we gave up great income or why we left steady employment or why we risk so much. We've had family and friends tell us we should quit or try something else. We had one friend tell us we should just go get a real job. Those words were like a knife piercing straight through our hearts. Sometimes the most discouraging words can come from those closest to you. It's not necessarily because they want to discourage you. They likely have your best interest in mind, but they don't understand the intimate details. Jimmy and I can talk to each other but sometimes we need someone else to confide in. The aloneness in our pursuit of God's plan has been more intense than any of the other pain or loneliness.

So, what do we do about the pain and loneliness? First, if the pain or loneliness is because someone has hurt you in any way, you have to forgive. I was facilitating a team building training several years ago. My client was dealing with a lot of workplace conflict, especially between three of the female employees. One portion of the training dealt with forgiveness. As I explained the physical, emotional, and relational impact of unforgiveness, one of the ladies spoke up and said, "I will never be able to forgive this person for what they have done. I don't care what it costs me. I didn't deserve what she did." Wow! She was very bitter and angry. Unforgiveness was already eating her alive. I wish I could say she saw the light and forgave and had a happy ending but she didn't. She alienated everyone so much her work performance was affected and she was eventually fired.

Unforgiveness is ugly and the only person it really hurts is the one not doing the forgiving.

After forgiveness, you need to give the pain to God. A couple years ago, I made a list of all of the things I was concerned about, the things breaking my heart. Then, every day I took one of the things on the list to God in prayer. I shared my heart in great detail with God and then I said 'God, _____ is yours. I trust you to take care of it.' I did this every day until I had given everything on my list to God. This was an energizing experience. It really freed up a lot of mental energy. When you give something to God to take care of, there is absolutely no reason to consume time or energy worrying about it. The creator of the universe has no problem taking care of every need, concern, worry, problem or illness. The big key is once you give it to God to walk away and leave it with him. In the future, when thoughts of the old things return, remind yourself of how you have given those old things to God and don't need to revisit them.

Chapter 2 – Spread it Out Before the Lord

2 Kings 19:14 After Hezekiah received the letter and read it, he went up to the LORD's Temple and spread it out before the LORD.

Hezekiah's story has become one of my favorites. I read it over and over, especially when I am in the middle of a battle that seems impossible. Have you been there? What I love is when everything happens at once. You know...financial struggles, sickness, spiritual attacks, a loved one dies, and then, to top it off you have a flat tire, break a nail or your kid gets a bad grade.

Hezekiah had one of those days. He received the letter from Sennacherib telling him of the other nations Assyria had conquered and how none of their gods saved them. Would God deliver Jerusalem? Hezekiah made the wisest decision possible at the time. He prayed. He told God what was going on. I can just picture him saying, "Here's what Sennacherib says.... Now God, we have got to have your help or we will not survive."

I believe Hezekiah had tremendous boldness and humility as he approached the Almighty. He had reverence for God and knew God was the supreme authority.

I can relate to Hezekiah because I was hurting physically and emotionally. I was utterly exhausted. God knew.

God, I'm desperate for you
I'm tired Lord
I can't do this anymore
I'm counting on you
Nothing is going right
I'm hurting
Frazzled
Exhausted
Alone
I feel abandoned
The pain is more than I can bear

There have been countless days when I have been ready to give up. During those times, I wonder if it is even worth the effort to go to the doctor, to take medicines, to try to get better. Is the ministry worth risking everything? How are we going to pay our bills this week? I get tired of trying to make things better. I don't want to give up. I don't want to quit. I don't want to be in pain. I don't want to live a miserable life.

Over and over I have "spread it out before the Lord." Not too long ago, I explained to the Lord how I was having a major melt down and just needed to talk, as if He didn't already know. As I told God everything that was hurting and overwhelming me, I felt such relief knowing the creator of the universe was listening to me. The moment I spilled my heart to God, I felt more peace than I had ever experienced in my life. Sometimes the challenges of life beat us down. Add spiritual battle and life can seem impossible. The ongoing day after day struggle can overwhelm us. But, God is always with us and He hears us when we call on Him.

Ephesians 6:11 Put on the full armor of God so that you can take your stand against the devil's schemes. 12 For

> *our struggle is not against flesh and blood, but against the rulers, against the authorities, against the powers of this dark world and against the spiritual forces of evil in the heavenly realms.*

I know many people do not understand the concept of a spiritual battle. Spiritual battle is real. There is a heaven and a hell and the forces of hell are in a war against God's army. Have you ever done something great for God – shared about Jesus with someone, taught a Sunday School class, gone on a missions trip, supported a missionary or church in a big way – followed by things going wrong in your life apparently for no reason? In all probability, you were in the middle of a spiritual battle designed to distract you and prevent you from being an effective follower of Christ. While there are no rules for battle (I'm not sure Satan follows rules.), patterns suggest spiritual battle takes place more intensely when you are doing or preparing to do something big for God. When we take a team with us for a missions project, one of the things we tell people is to be aware of distractions or things to come up to hinder participation in the project. We have a precious lady who volunteers to help us with some administrative work. We gave her the same speech we give all our volunteers. Later, she told us the week she started volunteering was the worst week of her life. Everything imaginable can happen to stop us from doing what God wants us to do. When you are facing hard times, be aware you may be in a spiritual battle.

Before I quit my job, every day was a tremendous struggle. Just the energy required to get up and get ready while dealing with the intense pain was almost more than I could tolerate. As I spread it out before the Lord one evening, all I could say was 'I'm hurting so bad and I'm so tired. Will you help me? I can't do this anymore.' Yet over and over God did give me the strength I needed for each day. He still does.

A few months ago, I was told about a woman fighting cancer and was given a couple of years to live. After prayer by several people, she went to the doctor and was told the cancer was in remission. There was no sign of cancer in her body. It is exciting to hear about God's wonderful miracles but I must admit I was a little jealous. How can God heal cancer but doesn't heal my RA or do a miracle with the funding we need for our ministry? I know He's able and I know He has done so much for us. There are just days when it seems like he's answering everyone else's prayers in huge ways. So, I spread it out before the Lord again. God says, "Be faithful, trust, obey."

> *Isaiah 40:28 Do you not know? Have you not heard? The Lord is the everlasting God, the Creator of the ends of the earth. He will not grow tired or weary, and his understanding no one can fathom.*

Maybe this is a place we all have to get to, each in our own way. For me, this is where I put my hands on my hips and say I'm not giving up. God has a plan and I am not going to be distracted. I'm not going to give up. It's not in my nature to give up. In fact, after I feel like giving up for a little while, I dig my heels in the ground and get a little sassy. Give me your best shot. You're not going to make me give up. My genius husband (he really is a genius) says, "We can't give up today. The answer may come tomorrow."

> *Psalm 73:1 Surely God is good to Israel, to those who are pure in heart. 2 But as for me, my feet had almost slipped; I had nearly lost my foothold. 3 For I envied the arrogant when I saw the prosperity of the wicked. 4 They have no struggles; their bodies are healthy and strong. 5 They*

are free from the burdens common to man; they are not plagued by human ills. 6 Therefore pride is their necklace; they clothe themselves with violence. 7 From their callous hearts comes iniquity; the evil conceits of their minds know no limits. 8 They scoff, and speak with malice; in their arrogance they threaten oppression. 9 Their mouths lay claim to heaven, and their tongues take possession of the earth. 10 Therefore their people turn to them and drink up waters in abundance. 11 They say, "How can God know? Does the Most High have knowledge?" 12 This is what the wicked are like— always carefree, they increase in wealth. 13 Surely in vain have I kept my heart pure; in vain have I washed my hands in innocence. 14 All day long I have been plagued; I have been punished every morning.

15 If I had said, "I will speak thus," I would have betrayed your children. 16 When I tried to understand all this, it was oppressive to me 17 till I entered the sanctuary of God; then I understood their final destiny. 18 Surely you place them on slippery ground; you cast them down to ruin. 19 How suddenly are they destroyed, completely swept away by terrors! 20 As a dream when one awakes, so when you arise, O Lord, you will despise them as fantasies.

21 When my heart was grieved and my spirit embittered, 22 I was senseless and ignorant; I was a brute beast before you. 23 Yet I am always with you; you hold me by my right hand. 24 You guide me with your counsel, and afterward you will take me into glory. 25 Whom have I in heaven but you? And earth has nothing I desire besides you. 26 My flesh and my heart may fail, but God is the strength of my heart and my portion forever. 27 Those who are far from you will perish; you destroy all who are unfaithful to you. 28 But as for me, it is good to be near God. I have made the Sovereign Lord my refuge; I will tell of all your deeds.

I love verses 16 and 17, "When I tried to understand all this, it was oppressive to me ***till I entered the sanctuary of God***." The Matthew Henry Complete Commentary on the Whole Bible explains how Asaph meditated on the attributes of God, consulted the scripture and prayed to God. [ii] What a great formula for us to use as we experience difficult times. When we are struggling to understand life, when things seem out of balance, confusing and unfair, entering the sanctuary of God brings clarity. When we focus on who God is and minimize who we are, we can breathe. We can see it is going to be ok. There is hope. Regardless of what is happening in our lives, God knows.

You can learn something about God from just about anything. I've learned a lot about God lately from carpet. I know it sounds silly. But, as I lay on the floor praying, I open my eyes and see the fibers and see God. Look at a piece of carpet. Look closely. What do you see? Hundreds of tiny fibers wound together, woven to make the larger piece. Each fiber is important to the overall end product. Imagine each person on the planet represents one fiber – each person that is, that was and that ever will be. When you look at the carpet, you don't really pay attention to the little tiny fibers, you look at the overall design, color, feel. God sees every one of those fibers – people. He sees me, loves me, hears me and knows my name. The same is true for you. Whoever you are, wherever you are, God sees you, loves you and knows your name. Nothing happens in this world that is a surprise to God. He's already seen it. He already knew it would happen. He knows what the result is going to be. He created the world. He is the Lord of Heaven's Armies. He is the King of all kings. He knows you.

God also has a plan for each of us. Each fiber plays a part in the overall big picture. Just like a runner would develop in a piece of carpet if fibers were cut or removed, we have a role in life and it matters if we miss it. Sometimes we just live life and forget or maybe we never pay attention to the fact God has a very specific, important plan for each one of us. What happens when we don't fulfill our role? Do others have to pitch in and do our part or does our part go undone? I don't know. I've often wondered. We will eventually find out. But, I definitely want to completely fulfill my role.

As Moses' successor, Joshua led the people of Israel into Canaan. He fought battles using strategies dictated by God. Joshua was wildly successful in conquering the territory God promised Israel. Joshua did everything God had asked. Can we say that?

Joshua 11:15 As the Lord commanded his servant Moses, so Moses commanded Joshua, and Joshua did it; he left nothing undone of all that the Lord commanded Moses.

As God looks at the carpet, He sees the design. The way one fiber interacts with another fiber, the result of layer upon layer of fibers connected in some way. He sees the different colors blending. He sees the beauty of each one of us doing what we are supposed to do and the results of what we do. If you've ever asked the question, "Do I matter?" the answer is unequivocally yes. We've got to find our place – our role – what it is God has for us to do. Spending time with God is the only way to find out. You can take quizzes, assessments, profiles, talk to counselors and on and on. But, the only thing that really matters is what you hear from God.

I get frustrated because God has a very specific plan for me but I feel horrible and don't have the energy to do what He's called me to do. My body and my heart are not always in sync. When I am struggling, I "spread it out before the Lord" more than any other time. My heart breaks when I don't have the strength to do what God has placed on my heart to do. For Hezekiah, God sent a message through Isaiah. Isaiah came to Hezekiah and said, "This is what the Lord, the God of Israel, says: I have heard your prayer ..." (2 Kings 19:20) He always hears and answers. Always. Sometimes we don't like the answer and other times we don't see the answer and sometimes the answer doesn't come right away. However, there is always an answer.

When you face challenges that seem unbeatable or you experience pain you believe you cannot endure, spread it out before the Lord. You can follow Hezekiah's example and literally spread out a letter to the Lord; I've done it exactly like Hezekiah. I wrote down what was bugging me, my physical pain, my concerns about our finances, needs for our ministry, everything. Then, I laid the letter in front of me and told the Lord how urgently I needed His help. You can also just sit down and tell the Lord exactly what is on your mind and how it makes you feel. What you say isn't going to shock Him. He already knows anyhow. If you've had a lousy day, tell God you've had a lousy day and explain what happened. We don't have to act super spiritual and talk in King James language. Just be yourself and talk to Him. Even though God already knows everything going on in your life, speaking the words is actually therapeutic. Visualize a jar full of marbles representing everything that went wrong. When you verbally share with God what is happening in your life, you are pouring the marbles out of the jar. You can now just let it go because it is in God's hands now.

After you express to God what is happening in your life, specifically ask Him for what you need. Does this mean you are automatically going to get what you want? No. God is not a genie waiting to grant your wishes. However, He is interested in hearing you ask. A perfect example of this is found in Mark 10:51. Jesus is traveling around Jericho with his disciples. As he is leaving the city, a blind man named Bartimaeus calls out to Jesus. Jesus, even though He knew what the man wanted, stopped and asked Bartimaeus what he wanted. Jesus wanted to hear what Bartimaeus had to say.

> *Mark 10:51 "What do you want me to do for you?" Jesus asked him. The blind man said, "Rabbi, I want to see."*

When I get to the point of asking God for what I want or what I perceive I need, I supplement my request with the following words: 'But God, what I really want is your will to be done. If this is a circumstance I must live through to learn something so I can be closer to you, then so be it. If this is part of your plan to get me where I need to be to fulfill what you've called me to do, then so be it. You have heard my request but my desire is to be perfectly in your will. I trust you.'

As you pour out your heart and spread it out before the Lord, He will hear you and He cares. What do you need to spread out before the Lord today? Why not spread it out right now?

Chapter 3 – Messages From God

Isaiah 43:2 When you go through deep waters and great trouble, I will be with you. When you go through rivers of difficulty, you will not drown! When you walk through the fire of oppression, you will not be burned up; the flames will not consume you. 3 For I am the LORD, your God, the Holy One of Israel, your Savior. (NLT)

I am humbled to think the Almighty creator even takes a millisecond to think about me. But, He does. Over and over. He hears me. He speaks to me. He answers my prayers. He really does know my name.

You would think literally having a household name, Kitchens, would be easy for people to understand. About 95 percent of the time when I am asked my name, I have to spell it at least three times before people get it. Seriously! Recently, we rented a U-Haul truck when we were moving all our belongings into storage. Jimmy brought the truck to our house. Then, Jimmy, Taylor and I loaded all of our boxes onto the truck. Our goal was to get the boxes unloaded and then, have the truck back at the house when our helpers arrived to load all the big stuff. Jimmy hops in the truck and it won't start. He calls customer service to get someone out to fix the truck. They promise someone will come in the next thirty minutes. Forty-five minutes later, no sign of the help. So, Jimmy calls again. He spends fifteen minutes, no exaggeration, trying to get the person to understand the last name of Kitchens. I was laughing so hard my sides hurt as I heard his side of the conversation:

> "Jimmy Kitchens. No, it's Kitchens. K..I..T..C..H..E.. N..S."
>
> "No, that's not it. K..I..T..C..H..E..N..S."
>
> "No, like the room in your house where you cook. You know, the kitchen."
>
> "K..I..T..C..H..E..N..S"
>
> "No, you know the room you cook in? Kitchens"
>
> "K..I..T..C..H..E..N..S"

This goes on for fifteen minutes. Finally, they got it and another hour later we finally received the help we needed. I'm so glad I don't have to go through all that with God. He knows me and He can spell Kitchens.

God is continually speaking to each of us. If you ever feel like God is silent, just spend some time listening. I had months in 2006 where I felt like God was ignoring me. I felt like He was silent and I would never hear His voice. I needed to be quiet and wait for Him to speak.

If we listen, God speaks to us in many different ways. I've always wanted to have a magical theophany type experience where God appears to talk to me like He did with Moses through the burning bush (Exodus 3). Instead, God has used His word, prayer, people, inner voice, songs and even nature to speak to me. Subtly, quietly and sometimes in my face with a big "hey I'm talking to you".

Have you ever read a scripture and even though you've read it many times before, this time it just jumps off the page and grabs you? When this happens, God is speaking to you through His written word. It seems to me the most frequent way God speaks to me is through a flow of unprompted, spontaneous thoughts or impressions usually while I'm being still during a time of prayer. When you believe you have heard a message from God, you need to process what you have heard and weigh it against God's word. God will never speak to us something contradictory to His written word.

God also uses other people to speak to us. On February 15, 2006, I was traveling to see one of my consulting clients. God seriously blessed me by putting her in my life. On this day, she spoke encouragement to me I so desperately needed. It had been one of those times when I didn't think I was physically going to survive. I was certain I was ready to lie down and die. The pain and fatigue were so bad I was in complete despair. Walking into her office building, my knees and hips hurt so severely I had to pull myself up the stairs with my hands on the handrail instead of pushing off of one foot to the other. Every step was a struggle. My friend began to tell me about some of her life experiences with her health, work and family. She shared with me how God used the pain in her life to slow her down and refocus on the important things, like her relationship with God and her family. We talked about the Bible studies we were each engaged in and we prayed for each other. Now, I don't know if you have been in a business office lately talking to a person in management but if you have you will recognize this is not normal business behavior. I fully believe God divinely appointed our meetings. While I was there to provide consulting and coaching, I received more than I gave. This day was a day when I needed to know someone was praying for me because I knew I didn't have another day in me.

After our meeting, I was weeping as I drove back home. I pleaded with God to help me. I wasn't even sure if I could make it home I was so exhausted. And then, randomly the song "Rest Easy" by Audio Adrenaline played on my mp3. The words brought hope. God began to speak to me through the song. I don't remember the rest of the hour drive home. I just remember hearing God's voice through the song.

> "Rest easy, have no fear. I love you perfectly, perfect love casts out fear. I'll take your burden, you take my grace. Rest easy in my embrace."[iii]

The very next Sunday at church, God spoke to me again. He said, "I keep my promises. I was there when the doctor gave you the news. I was there when you cried yourself to sleep. I was there when the pain was so bad. No matter how lonely you feel, I am there."

One thing I have learned is in order to hear God I have to be quiet! For some of us being quiet is harder than for others. My mind is always moving. There is always noise in my head. I'm thinking about things, planning for what's next, and on and on. Even when I pray, I have to make a conscious effort to make my mind be quiet. I ask God to still my mind so I can hear Him. It took some time to create the habit but now I find myself throughout the day asking God to still my mind. Just like He spoke "peace" to the stormy waters and they were calm, He can do the same for our minds. And when our minds are calm, quiet, and still, we can hear His voice and His heart beat.

God's primary source for speaking to us is His written word. About fifteen years ago, a lady at church came to me and Jimmy and told us the Lord had given her a scripture for us. At the time I really didn't think much of it. However, as years have gone by, God has reminded me over and over. It has become a foundation for me.

Joshua 1:6 Be strong and courageous, because you will lead these people to inherit the land I swore to their forefathers to give them.

I never realized how much I take God's written word for granted until my first trip to China. Our team smuggled in Bibles – the Chinese Fire Bible. When we gave the Bibles to the preachers and pastors, they literally hugged the Bibles close to their chests. I can't even put into words the expressions on their faces, the reverence, the amazement, the joy. It was precious to them, like an expensive jewel. It challenged me. It stirred my heart. God is speaking to us through His word. He has messages for each of us in His word.

Most of my life, I felt inadequate, unlovable, totally dissatisfied with me. I had confidence in my abilities at work, as a leader in business and in our ministry. In every other way, I saw myself as a total failure. At 110 pounds, I thought I was fat. I always compared myself to others and was never good enough. I would have great successes in life but still saw it as not good enough. I was especially insecure when I was around other ministers' wives. I dreaded any interaction and meetings with other ministers' wives. It terrified me.

My first missions trip was to Jamaica in 2004. It was a women's ministry team from our state. You guessed it ... ministers' wives and church women and me. I immediately began comparing myself to the other people on the trip. I don't pray as eloquently as this one and I don't talk as impressively as that one and our church wasn't as big as this church. Then, I thought I'm so insignificant. My natural response was to shrink back – to not do things I knew I could do, to not stand out (just like my junior high days). If you knew me, you would know this behavior is so not me now! I am usually a take charge, be in the middle of everything, talk to everybody leader. But, not this time. I felt so worthless and insignificant. I needed to see who I am through God's eyes.

God uses the craziest things to get our attention. Part of the Jamaica trip involved driving across the island to Montego Bay for a women's retreat. After facilitating the day and a half retreat, our team headed back to Christiana. The drive from Montego Bay to Christiana was curvy, bouncy and made a bunch of us really car sick. Of course, I was one of them. I was horrified, embarrassed and my mind conjured up old memories of my childhood fears. Along with the car sickness, my RA was totally out of control. I was in so much pain I could barely stand up and I could not walk without help. One of my new friends walked me to my room. I climbed in bed with my clothes on and she helped me get my jewelry off. My hand was so swollen we couldn't get my bracelet off. I laid there and cried. She comforted me. I told her I feel like such a wimp. She told me I wasn't a wimp. She also said, "You inspire me. You sacrifice so much. People are watching you." She wiped my tears. This moment impacted me in a huge way. Instead of ridicule, I received compassion. I didn't know I was worth compassion. Someone saw me as valuable. God used my new friend to tell me I was worthwhile.

One night in Jamaica, we had a time of prayer. I remember feeling like I was in the way rather than being a part of. Although God used my friend to tell me I was worthwhile, my mind was still toying with the idea I was insignificant. After praying for a couple of people, I just sat in my seat and prayed silently. I can't describe exactly what I was thinking or feeling but I felt pretty disheartened. As I sat there, God spoke these things to me: trust me; it's ok to be persistent; listen; lift up your head my daughter. My view of who I am changed at this moment. God called me His daughter. If I'm the King of King's daughter, then, I must matter. Something happened within me at that instant. I wrote in my journal:

I am your daughter and I will lift my head. No longer will I bow to self-criticism or doubt. You have made me and called me. I trust you.

This became a pledge for me to reinvent my life. Life changed for me at this time. Not only did I see me in a new way, my relationships became stronger. I feel like since 2004 my relationship with Jimmy has been better than ever. Sure there are still times when we get frustrated with each other but I finally feel really close. I let people in my life differently than before. My friendships have significantly more depth. I can honestly say I am happy with who I am now. In fact, I love who God has made me. I could have never said those words before the summer of 2004. I wish it wouldn't have taken 34 years for me to get there.

It's funny how God works sometimes. One day in January 2009, I wrote as my Facebook status, "DeAnna is wishing I hadn't opened all the mail last night. Sometimes ignorance is bliss...=)." I normally try to be positive in my status but I just had the urge to say exactly what I felt at the moment. Around midnight, I was playing a game on my computer when one of my cousins started chatting with me. She saw my status and responded to it. After chatting a while on Facebook, she asked me to call her. We talked and prayed together for almost an hour. This spontaneous intense prayer when I was going through a hard time was just what I needed. We encouraged each other and God spoke to both of us in powerful ways. She said things to me I needed to hear and confirmed what I had been feeling God directing me to do. This encounter was something neither of us expected or planned. But something I will never forget.

God is not limited in how He works. He uses things we see as trivial as much as He uses the grand, maybe even more. Let God speak to you. Be obedient. Hear the prompting He gives you. Then, watch and be amazed at what He does. If we truly want to hear God's heart beat, we must be listening for Him.

Looking back on my life, I wouldn't change a thing. Every trial, problem, heartache, joy, blessing, hurt, pain all have made me who I am. I can see God's hand, even through the dark times, molding me, breaking me, rebuilding me to be who He wants me to be.

When you are in a place where you need to hear from God, tell Him. Lord, help me listen to you and hear your voice and be courageous to do what you want. Reveal to me what you want me to learn from this situation.

I am constantly amazed how such a big God cares about the things in our lives. He wants to be involved in our lives. He desires to be close to us. He wants to hear us and speak to us. I am living my life in great anticipation and expectation for what God is going to do. Most of my life to this point has been more of wondering what God will do or wondering if God will do something. There's no power or freedom there. There is an abundance of power and freedom in living life as if God's already done what He's promised. Live with anticipation and expectation. Walk in victory not despair. Expect. Don't be surprised when you see the answer. God always keeps His word.

God always has our best interest in mind. He sees where we are, where we're going, where He wants us and every option for every choice we will ever have to make. Wow! God is so good! He is amazing. He knows – wherever you are right now, He knows. He is not blinded. He is not unaware. He knows and He cares. He is speaking.

God leads us to the places in life where we need to be to fulfill the plan He has for our lives. God Almighty wants each of His precious daughters (and sons) to be wildly successful in fulfilling everything He created us for. Not only does He call us, He teaches us everything we need to know and develops the abilities we need to fulfill His plan.

In June 2008, God began speaking to me about not going on our summer trip to Monterrey, Mexico. At first, I was a little confused because we've felt like we were all supposed to go together as a family. As I continued to pray, God made it clear I was supposed to stay home to pray and fast. This was the beginning of an amazing journey with my King.

In July 2008, we had made the decision to sell our house. We listed two days before Jimmy left for Mexico. In those two days, the three of us worked non-stop to 'stage' the house. The next two days, Taylor and I continued the work, packing and deep cleaning everything. We were physically beat up and worn down. Emotionally, I was drained. We were out of money and seemingly out of time. After Jimmy left, Taylor and I were working to finish getting the house ready to show. It seemed like every few minutes one more thing was going wrong. Let me preface the next statement by saying – I hate going to Wal-Mart about as much as I hate going to the dentist. When I was pulling into the Wal-Mart parking lot for the 4th time in 12 hours at 11:00 at night in the rain, I just began begging God to please help us - not only was I frustrated at all the problems but I was in tears because I had to buy stuff to fix the house and didn't know where the money was going to come from. Rain was pouring from the sky with lightening flashes every few seconds. This was a perfect moment for some thriller movie music. The day had been so frustrating I sat in my car and asked God to please not let me get struck by lightning as I'm walking into the store! I'm laughing now - I wasn't then. I truly felt like I had a high probability of being struck by lightning as I walked from the car to the store. Fortunately, I was wrong.

On the following Sunday, I had already determined if the opportunity was given to ask for prayer, I was going to ask. I was so overwhelmed with our life situation I couldn't verbalize anything. But, I know God knew. Right before the pastor prayed for me, a lady spoke a prophetic word.

"It is done. Just believe." That's all she said. These days of preparing the house to sell led up to my prayer and fasting time while Jimmy was in Monterrey. This was an amazing time and has set in motion growth and depth that truly overwhelms me.

During these two weeks, I had a different prayer focus each day. The first day, my focus was on thanksgiving for what God has done for me. I wrote a list of 155 things to thank God for. I put my total focus on that day on thanking God for what He's done and what I trust Him to do. Another day, I focused on praising God for who He is. I am continually increasing in awe of God's greatness. When I think of who God is, I am overwhelmed by his bigness. I am so small and frail compared to His bigness. Thank God; He is big. Help me to keep me in proper perspective.

> *Psalm 91: 1 Those who live in the shelter of the Most High will find rest in the shadow of the Almighty. 2 This I declare of the LORD: He alone is my refuge, my place of safety; he is my God, and I am trusting him. 3 For he will rescue you from every trap and protect you from the fatal plague. 4 He will shield you with his wings. He will shelter you with his feathers. His faithful promises are your armor and protection.*

I frequently pray these verses from Psalm 91. God really does have great things for each of us. As I read the words "His faithful promises," I wonder exactly what God has promised me. I know there are a lot of promises in the Bible. Are the promises just for those in the time and setting in the Bible or are they for me? I wonder sometimes if I have taken ownership of a promise intended for only a specific time and person instead of for all mankind. In this state of wonderment, I asked God to start revealing promises that include me. What is it God has promised me? As I asked this question and integrated it into my prayer time (listening for God to speak to me), I began a list of what God is speaking to me and promising me. What is God saying to you? Write it down and go back to it often.

My prayer journal is one of my most precious belongings. I keep it with me all the time. It's a simple notebook small enough to carry with me. It's divided into four sections. First, is my prayer list. I listed all of my family, friends, missionaries, people who support Clear Vision Ministries and our volunteers. This list is several pages long. Second, I listed needs for Clear Vision Ministries. This is just one page. Then I have about 4 things listed for me personally. I intentionally arranged my prayer list in this order and with more focus on others than on me. The second section includes a list of who God is, then, a list of what God has done for me. I use this section as I worship God for who he is and what he's done for me. The third section is scriptures that have special meaning for me. I have handwritten them in my journal and I read or pray them out loud. Finally, the last section is where I write down what God is speaking to me. If you don't journal, I highly recommend getting started. Journaling allows you to capture on paper what you are experiencing in life, what you're praying for, what God is speaking to you about and records answers to prayer. I've looked back numerous times at old journals and am encouraged each time as I see in black and white what God has done in my life.

Realize God speaks to each of us in a way we, individually, can understand. He does what we need at the time. God sees the big picture. So, He knows how our current situation fits with our future. God knew I needed to hear what my friend would say in Jamaica, even if it meant I would have to be sick in order to hear it. God has been speaking since the beginning of the world and He hasn't stopped. We just need to listen so we can hear the message He has for us.

Chapter 4 – Knowing God

Exodus 6:2 God also said to Moses, "I am the Lord. 3 I appeared to Abraham, to Isaac and to Jacob as God Almighty, but by my name the Lord I did not make myself known to them.

I am completely astounded at how God Almighty wants us to know Him and He wants to know us. As we read through scripture, we are not only given descriptions of who He is but we are given His name. Through a variety of experiences in Old Testament times, God's name is revealed. Some of His names are below, each one with a specific meaning illuminating who God is.

- He is El Shaddai, God Almighty, the most powerful. The Lord appeared to Abram (Genesis 17:1) and told him "I am God Almighty." He is absolutely able to do anything. Try to imagine a challenge to God's power he could not meet. How does the thought that nothing can challenge God's power encourage you and build your view of God and faith in God?
- He is Adonai, Master. God is the master and authority. In Joshua 5:14, Joshua bows facedown to reverence of Adonai. Joshua then asks Adonai what message

He has for His servant. We are servants of the Most High Master.

- He is El Olam, the Everlasting God. He is completely inexhaustible. He doesn't go away or wear out. He never ceases to exist. He's everlasting. God doesn't have a birthday and death day – He's eternally infinite. (Isaiah 26:4)
- He is Jehovah Jireh, the Lord our Provider. Nothing is out of His reach. There is no dollar figure bigger than God. There is no need greater than the capacity God has to provide. Abraham calls God Jehovah Jireh when He provides a ram as a substitute for the sacrifice of Isaac, Abraham's son. (Genesis 22:14)
- He is Jehovah Nissi, the Lord our Banner. He is our rallying point. In the old days different factions carried flags. If there was trouble, there was a rallying cry and everyone would gather at their flag and fight together against the enemy. God is the rallying point to turn a hopeless situation into a victory. (Exodus 17:15)
- He is Jehovah Shalom, the Lord our Peace. He is where we find peace and rest even in the midst of a battle. As the Lord was directing Gideon to go to battle with the Midianites, Gideon is afraid and giving numerous excuses to the Lord of why he cannot go to battle. After conversing for a while, the Lord tells Gideon to not be afraid. Gideon calls the Lord Jehovah Shalom – his Peace. (Judges 6:24)
- He is Jehovah Sabbaoth, the Lord of Hosts. He is the commander of heaven's armies and He is royalty. Imagine the most powerful commander-in-chief merged with the most majestic of all royalty. This name is used over 285 in the Bible. (1 Samuel 17:45, Isaiah 6:3)

- He is Jehovah Tsidkenu, the Lord our Righteousness. Jehovah Tsidkenu restores man's relationship to God. Through Jesus Christ we are made righteous. It is through the Lord our Righteousness we are made clean and holy in the sight of God. (Jeremiah 23:6)
- He is Jehovah Ro'i, the Lord our Shepherd. He cares for His people as a shepherd cares for his sheep. As our Shepherd, Jehovah Ro'i protects us, shows kindness to us, helps us, cleans us, feeds us, serves us and gives us loyal love. David describes the Lord our Shepherd in Psalm 23.
- He is Jehovah Shammah, the Lord is There. He is present with us at all times sovereignly accomplishing His purposes. He does not abandon us or hide from us. Jehovah Shammah is dwelling with us – living with us. We are never alone. (Ezekiel 48:35)
- He is Jehovah Rapha, the Lord that Heals. (Exodus 15:26)Jehovah Rapha restores our physical, mental, relational and emotional health. He is our healer.
- He is YHWH, I AM. He is self-existent, he is eternal, unchangeable. In Exodus 3:13, Moses asks who he should say sent him to Egypt to lead the Israelites out of Egypt. In Exodus 3:14, God responds and tells Moses His name is I AM. He is not dependent on any other being for His own existence. [iv]

Even though we may know the names of God and have an understanding of where each one came from and what it means, we will never truly internalize it until we experience God in our own life. We may know God heals; we may have heard testimonies of people He has healed; He may have even healed someone close to us; BUT we will not truly know Him as our healer until He heals us – you – me. We may have read God is our banner and understand it means He is our rallying point, our hope in battle, He has unfurled Himself as a banner in front of us and behind us and on top of us to stop the arrows from piercing us BUT until we are in a battle, we will not really understand what it means for God to be my banner. I have learned God is our banner, God is our provider, our peace, our strength and He is with us through everything. It is through our trials we can internalize who God is: my protector, provider, shield, banner, savior, peace, joy, best friend, gracious, mighty, prayer-answering, majestic.

God called us to start Clear Vision Ministries (CVM) in 2000. The vision God gave us is to work with missionaries, pastors and local churches in developing and third world countries. Using my consulting and business background and Jimmy's pastoral and leadership background, we created our strategic plan, articles of incorporation, constitution and by-laws. So we had down on paper what God had called us to do. Over the next few years we waited for God's timing for us to actually start doing the work. The more time we focused on CVM, the more battles we faced ranging from health to finances and more. In these intense battles, we have seen God work as Jehovah Nissi, our banner. When we feel beat down and out of hope, we see the Lord our Banner and know we are not defeated. Because He has protected us from the attacks that would have destroyed us, I have an unshakable confidence in God. I know I can count on Him. Even when circumstances are bleak, I can look up and see the Banner and run to Him and be safe.

~God Reigns~

In those times when life happens – when things don't go as planned, when disaster strikes, when storms rise, when everything looks impossible – we can choose to know God or to become inwardly focused. I've done my share of looking inward, feeling sorry for myself, wondering what I did to deserve "this." We all have dark times. If we're not careful we can be so focused on ourselves and circumstances we forget who God really is. We can turn dark times into black holes sucking life from our very existence.

Psalm 139:12 even the darkness will not be dark to you; the night will shine like the day, for darkness is as light to you.

It's a good thing God doesn't strike us with lightening every time we have a meltdown! Sometimes, I have to whack myself on the back of the head and remind myself I know better. What I know is we always have a choice in how we respond to life.

During one of those weeks where I just felt slammed on all sides, God reminded me of the Sunday School class Jimmy and I taught on expanding our view of God. We looked at the names of God, the story behind each name and what it meant to us. We were following it up with a few weeks on how to respond to what we had learned about who God is. One of those follow-up lessons focused on our response in difficult times. Our response is always a choice. We can run to God our banner as we seek to rally in a battle or we can try to champion the battle ourselves. We can rely on God our provider or we can do it on our own. We can allow hard times to grow us or we can let them defeat us.

James 1:2-4 Consider it pure joy, my brothers, whenever you face trials of many kinds, because you know that the testing of your faith develops perseverance. Perseverance must finish its work so that you may be mature and complete, not lacking anything.

The truth is God reigns over everything. If we hadn't been in desperate situations, we would not have known

God as our provider, peace, banner...I'm glad I know Him that way even if the process to get there was hard. I can't tell you how many times we've told God we're not sure we can survive another day. He responds by saying, just trust me. Run with endurance. The battle is won – you may not see it yet, but it's won.

There will always be times in our lives where it seems like the world is crashing in around us. Even in those times, God still reigns. It's His world. He knows what's going on. Nothing is a surprise to Him. He understands our pain. He recognizes our fear. He hears our heart's cry. He reigns. Nothing can conquer Him. He has complete ultimate authority over everything in our lives. I'm in one of those times right now where I have to rely on my knowledge that God is in control and nothing is too difficult for Him. It's too much for me. I can't handle it. God can. God reigns. He carries every one of my burdens for me. He supplies every ounce of strength I need. When I feel I can't take another step, He takes the step for me. God reigns. Do we really live like we believe God reigns?

~Learning a Few Lessons~

God has been teaching me to be thankful for the lessons I am learning. Sometimes life lessons are not the most enjoyable experiences. In fact, many times the way we learn the lesson is through tremendous difficulties. The difficulties leading to lessons will ultimately lead to our growth as a person and as a follower of Christ if we learn from it.

One of the lessons God is teaching me is endurance through intense trials. I have been so tempted to just give up but I can't. I have to endure because God endures. His love endures forever – his mercy is unending – his grace is eternal – he is always faithful – he always hears me – he is always with me – his power will not cease – his authority is supreme – he has always been and will always be. So, I can't quit. I can't give up. I have to believe. I have to have faith and trust in him.

I've also been learning lessons of trusting God, letting go of the controls, being still and many more. If you really look at Jesus in the gospels, He spends a lot of time teaching people, especially His disciples. He's the best teacher who has ever existed. The critical factor is how willing we are to be taught.

In my career as a consultant and trainer, I encountered people who were eager to learn new skills and improve their performance and capabilities. I also encountered people who had no interest in learning anything. They didn't want to improve; in fact, they saw no need to learn anything. You can spot the latter pretty easy. They are the people who sit at the back of the classroom glaring at you with their arms crossed and foot tapping. Ok, not all of the non-interested people are that obvious but it doesn't take long to figure out if a person wants to learn. I unequivocally believe every person has room to learn and grow. There is no human who has learned everything. I'm not just talking about book knowledge. The growing process also includes behaviors and character development. We develop our character most deeply through our experiences in life. If we allow God to work, He will use those life experiences to teach us.

To facilitate personal growth, we must be teachable. Being teachable means we are willing to admit we don't know everything and we are willing to change whatever needs to change in order to learn and grow. A key ingredient for teachableness is humility. Pride prohibits learning.

We also need to recognize when we are being taught a lesson. Sometimes it is hard to identify when God is teaching us. We may be going through a hard time and never stop to think about what we are learning. We may be in the middle of the best time of our life, absolutely full of hope, joy, peace, success and not realize God is teaching us. Really the key is making a deliberate effort to stop and think about our life and God. Do you see a pattern of events or behaviors – good, bad, or even neutral? Do you experience intense emotions during certain situations? Do you hear God speaking to you in a new way? Do you have a peaked interest in a deeper relationship with God?

Once we recognize God is trying to teach us something, we have a choice in how we respond to the lesson. We can respond by doing nothing or by absorbing it and applying it. Repeatedly, I've seen people have to repeat lessons because they did not learn or apply what God was teaching them. You may know someone who is in a cycle of repeating the same life experiences over and over again. I have a friend who has repeated the same lesson for years. Unfortunately, her lesson has involved some pretty significant emotional and relationship pain. Instead of trusting in God and being obedient, she has given in to family pressure. She has lived for years with hurt, depression and dissatisfaction with her life and relationships. I talked to her many times and she told me specifically what God wanted her to learn, but it was "too hard" or "too uncomfortable." So, she chose the path of least resistance but more pain.

Learning is generally not a comfortable process. Learning can be extremely humbling. Have you ever experienced growing pains? I remember as a kid having pain in my shins. Disappointingly, the growing pains in my shins did not result in significant growth! I only made it to 5'2". Nevertheless, the growth caused pain. In behavioral, intellectual, spiritual and relational growth, you will experience discomfort. The discomfort may seem unbearable at times but if you endure and apply what you are learning it will be worthwhile.

~Power in Praise~

Several years ago, I did what I called a "praise fast." Basically, this involved spending a month thanking God and praising Him instead of asking for things. When I had a need, I would thank God instead of asking for His help. Another part of this "praise fast" was as I read the Bible to write down every reason I saw to thank God. My list was several pages long. During this time, God did some amazing things in my life. I learned to be grateful for life in a deep way. There are a lot of things we take for granted. God could have created a world in black and white instead of the colorful world we live in. God didn't have to give us noses to smell the sweet fragrances of flowers or my son's favorite scent – pie. The point is not to praise God to get something but to change my focus to who He is and have a thankful heart. I have repeated the "praise fast" many times since then and each time I am in awe of what God does in me. When our focal point is the majesty and greatness of God and all of the things we are thankful for, our attitudes, our behaviors and our desires change. Praising God can transform everything about us if we allow it. What are you thankful for?

> *Acts 16:25 About midnight Paul and Silas were praying and singing hymns to God, and the other prisoners were listening to them. 26 Suddenly there was such a violent earthquake that the foundations of the prison were shaken. At once all the prison doors flew open, and everybody's chains came loose.*

At the end of 2006, God was stirring me – actually, it felt like I was in a food processor on the high setting! I had had enough of me. I was tired of everyone focusing on my physical health instead of me as a person. I was tired of being sick. I was tired of the battles we were fighting in order to raise funds for CVM. But more than anything, I was tired of my focus being on me. I needed less of me and more of God. I remember at the end of a Sunday morning service, as the Pastor was beginning his closing prayer, I went up to the altar area and knelt down on the floor. Sobbing, I prayed for God to break me. God, I want more of you and less of me. Help me to become less so you can become more. Then immediately after I began to think "Break me — what on earth have I just asked for!!" I needed to be broken so I could get rid of the things holding me back.

Over and over I have prayed for God to be glorified so people would see Him, not me, in the things I do and for Him to do things through me I could not do on my own. What I do in life is not about me and I never want it to be. About four years ago, God impressed in my spirit through this horrible rheumatoid arthritis disease, He would receive glory; I will experience Him as my strength because I will have none on my own and the things I do will be because of Him not because of me. I have seen this come true over and over. I cannot tell you how many times I could not stand up on my own but God gave me strength enough to do the work I had to do. There were countless times when I was so sick and exhausted because of my medication I could not complete a thought in my head, but was able to consult with a company on how to improve their organizational structure – and the recommendations worked. The first time I was shocked. I couldn't even remember what I told them to do.

For a long time, I thought God giving me strength was the complete definition of "He would do things through us we could not do on our own." Then it clicked one night. Creating a business structure, developing a board of directors, networking, marketing, web design, video development, putting together teams, leading teams, managing projects, counseling, coaching, troubleshooting and providing support to missionaries – those were all things

Jimmy and I had skills, education and experience in doing on our own. Yes, God gave us the ability to do those things but we had done it all before in some way. Now, we have done everything we know how to do. We have maxed out our own abilities. We have reached the limit on our own knowledge. We have read everything we can find to read and used every skill we have. Now, we are beyond what we can do on our own. This is the trusting God phase of this journey. Now, we don't know what to do. Now, God can show us who He really is! I cannot tell you how amazingly exciting this is. What does He have in store? Now, the adventure can really begin. It is all a big surprise now. We have done all of the strategic planning, goal setting, delegating, blah, blah, blah. (Which I fully believe is still important.) But now, our lives and ministry are truly in God's hands. There is nothing either of us can do beyond what we have already done. What will God do? I can't wait to find out!

> *James 1:2-4 Consider it pure joy, my brothers, whenever you face trials of many kinds, because you know that the testing of your faith develops perseverance. Perseverance must finish its work so that you may be mature and complete, not lacking anything.*

~Pursued by God~

I crave more of God. More intense than a craving for food or a need for friendship or cure for disease, my heart craves more of God. I am captivated by His presence. I'm overwhelmed by His mercy, grace, compassion, favor, greatness beyond measure. If we ever think we have reached complete intimacy with God, we are fooled. There is always more.

Hosea 2:14 Therefore I am now going to allure her; I will lead her into the desert and speak tenderly to her.

I am profoundly moved every time I read this verse. Hosea and Gomer's story is one of the most amazing love stories ever. If you have ever felt abandoned, rejected, betrayed or unloved, this is a must read story. The Lord tells Hosea to marry an adulterous wife and raise her illegitimate children. I think I would pause at that point and ask the Lord if He had lost His mind! Why in the world would you want to start a relationship with someone you knew would not be trustworthy; someone who would betray you. Hosea obeyed and married Gomer. True to her nature, Gomer was unfaithful to Hosea. She had three illegitimate children. After she has been unfaithful, God describes her punishment. Then comes verse 14, saying regardless of what she's done, I am going to allure her. He's going to speak to her heart in a way to win her over. He will speak tenderly to her. I think of times when Jimmy has come up behind me, held me and spoke softly in my ear, tenderly. Can you picture God speaking in this fashion to Gomer? It's a beautiful picture. We are relentlessly pursued by God. He is persistent, unyielding, insistent, ruthless, uncompromising in His pursuit.

After the Lord talks about alluring Gomer, he tells Hosea to go find her and show his love to her again. Hosea finds his wife. Gomer had become the slave of her lover. Then Hosea buys her back. Wow! He essentially is buying back what was already his. Jesus paid the price for each of us.

Through whatever means, God wants everyone to know how much he loves them. He wants to share his magnificence with all human beings. He wants to use us to convey his relentlessly pursuing love for them. How? He'll do whatever it takes, including buying back what is already His. God uses each one of us – those who are willing – to share His relentless love.

In Ecuador and Honduras, He used a clown to play with kids and make balloons to show His love. In the fall of 2008, we were on the Galapagos Island of San Cristobal. Taylor and I led part of our team in doing a Kids Club. The Kid's Club team went out on Monday to the schools and soccer fields to invite kids to come to the church for the Club de Niños. Tico the clown (a.k.a. Taylor) and some of the other team members made animal balloons and gave them to the kids. Each afternoon at the Club de Niños, we played games, learned a Bible verse, had a puppet skit, gave out prizes and had a lot of fun playing with the kids. The first afternoon, we had about 75 kids and about 10 parents. On the third day, we had over 120 kids and parents! The kids had so much fun. They laughed and played and learned about Jesus. On the Wednesday night, Pastor Wilson wanted to have a closing service with the team. When we arrived at the church, there were 12 boys from the Club de Niños at the church. We thought they would leave when they realized there was no clown, puppets, games, or prizes. But, they stayed, listened and participated in everything we did. At the end of the night, the boys all gave Taylor a big group hug. As they did, he prayed over them for God to make them the men of the church and for Him to use these boys. The next week, we saw Pastor Wilson. He told us that on Sunday there were 30 kids from the kids club at church. They were all asking for Tico. Pastor Wilson said the parents stood outside the building and listened. When church was over, he talked to the parents and they were pleased with what their kids were learning. Someone in the church bought a clown outfit for the pastor. He told the kids to come back on Friday for Club de Niños. God used a clown to relentlessly pursue His beloved children.

In China, he used a crazy bunch of Americans to show His love to a tour guide who committed his life to Jesus. In Romania, He is using flannel graphs in the pastor's message to illustrate His pursuit. We are a part of His love story. You are a part of His love story. How is God using you to show His love to the world?

One of the things I enjoy so much about our mission's projects is our team devotions. I love the intense worship and prayer and seeing God move. I have seen God in such amazing ways. The only way I can describe it is that it makes me feel full, complete, rich and completely at peace. The cool thing is God wants us to be with Him like that every day. It is easy to have deep intimate time with God when we are away from our normal routine. When we are enveloped in the chaos of life, we can so easily let our nearness to God slip away.

God has made himself known to me by giving peace in bad situations, by answering prayers, by allowing me to sense His presence, by speaking to me through His word and in my heart. He gives me a continually growing desire to pursue Him as He pursues me. Picture a scene from a movie where a man and woman in love see each other after some time away from each other. They look across the room or parking lot or airport or spaceship to see their beloved and start running toward each other arms wide open. Both people are moving. Each is pursuing the other. God is running toward each of us with His arms wide open.

God is greater than all things. He is in control at all times. When things seem impossible, He makes a way. He is all powerful and all knowing. He is everything I need. He is my foundation and my protection. He is my strength and my hope. Because God is my solid foundation, nothing can blow me down – no matter how big the storm – because He is greater. God is my strength and he will help me and uphold me. He has called me and he will be with me no matter what.

God is on my side and nothing will prevail against Him. This amazing God is the one who is pursuing us.

As Americans, we don't really understand the majesty, authority and power of a king. We really have no reference for grasping what a king is outside of history, stories, books and movies. A king is much more than a fairy tale, grander than a story, more magnificent than a blockbuster movie can portray. We serve the king of all kings. Jesus is greater than any king who has ever been or ever will be. He has all power, all authority, unimaginable majesty.

Show me your glory in a way you design for me.
In my weakness, help me to show your strength.
In my pain, help me to show your grace.
In my fatigue, help me to show your hope.
I would rather feel bad every day of my life and worship you, God, and be in your presence than to have one day, one moment, without you and be in perfect health.
In my brokenness, let there be a sweet fragrance of worship released. Break me and empty me of me and fill me up with all of you.
God of wonders,
Full of majesty,
Giver of all good things,
Eternal father,
Keeper,
Savior,
Sustainer,
Life,
Hope,
Peace,
Joy,
The answer,
The truth,
The only way,

The reason,
The why,
The how,
You reign forever,
You conquer it all,
Nothing can stop you,
Nothing is bigger than you,
Nothing can compare to you,
You rule,
You reign,
You rescue,
You are everything,
You are my hope.

The more I discover about God and the more I experience God, the more I want of Him. Sometimes all I can do is just lay at His feet and worship Him. God is so amazing. We only see a speck of who is. He is so worthy of our worship, reverence, devotion. When I stop and think about who God is and what He's done for me, I am totally overwhelmed. There is no one who loves us the way God loves us. He has given us everything we need. He cherishes His children.

As we experience God, as He speaks to us, as He works in our lives, we should always respond. The actions of God demand a response. He doesn't speak to hear His own voice. He doesn't call us as a game. He doesn't grace us with His presence for dramatic effect. He acts; we respond. He speaks; we listen and obey. He calls; we do. He is present; we worship.

I thank God for helping me to realize the positive things resulting from my physical struggles:

- Courage
- Resolve
- Faith
- Greater trust

- Total surrender to God
- Freedom in worship
- Reliance on God not on me
- Daily miracles
- Meaningful relationships
- Opening up to others
- Blessings through others
- Teaching opportunities
- Freedom to take risks
- Clear focus on what's important
- Creativity
- Glimpse of God's strength and compassion
- Sympathy and empathy and compassion for others
- Realization of who I am in God
- Ability to think about what I think, do and say
- Gratitude
- Opportunity to see God working every day

As I get to know God in new and deeper ways, I am driven to go even deeper. What can I let go of so I can be closer to God? What can I rearrange in my life so I have more intensity in my relationship with my King? Sometimes we need to give up stuff; sometimes we need to just make time. Sometimes we have to be willing to give up everything. Whatever it is, it's never a wasted sacrifice.

However much you know God, you haven't fully known Him yet. Our knowledge of Him and intimacy with Him is not complete yet. There is so much more. It reminds me of one of our trips to Honduras. After a very lengthy layover at the Roatan, Honduras airport that was mysteriously over as soon as the soccer game ended, our team began to load the plane. As we walked out on the tarmac, we saw our luggage. We even touched our luggage as we walked by. When we arrived in La Ceiba, our luggage was mysteriously missing. We saw it, touched it but did not have possession of it in the end. There was an encounter with the luggage but it was not enough. An encounter only lasts for a brief time.

Know God. The more you know Him, the <u>more you trust Him</u>, the more intimate your relationship is, the more you want to know Him. He is habit forming! When we know Him and trust him and place our focus on Him – our problems and circumstances may not change but our view of the circumstances in light of who God is WILL CHANGE.

When you are at your best and at your worst, there is no one else who cares as much as He does. I know without any hesitation He is the only reason I have survived the last three years. He is my constant source of hope and strength. As the Lord allured Gomer, He is also alluring you. He is relentlessly pursuing you – His beloved.

Chapter 5 – Waiting Kind of Feels Like Being Lazy

Psalm 27:14 Wait for the Lord; be strong, and let your heart take courage; wait for the Lord!

If you haven't figured it out already, I am a very driven, type-A, get things done person. I like to see results. I like to feel productive. So, for me, waiting on God feels like I'm being incredibly lazy. It would be easier for me if He gave me a to-do list, instead of saying "wait and trust me".

I guess it is truthfully about control – me letting go of it and letting God have it. Life is a little more comfortable when I'm in control. I'm learning to be content with God being in control and me letting go of the reins.

Waiting. Hmm. It's hard to do but oh so worth it. One of my "company" dinners is my slow cooked Plum Herb Brisket. It is delish! The key is the 4-6 hour slow cooking process. If you rush it, the meat isn't as flavorful or as tender. When you allow the flavors to soak in and the meat to cook slowly, you end up with a melt-in-your-mouth entrée. Life is kind of similar. When we rush through life, decisions, time with God or time with our family, we end up with a cheap imitation of what it could be if we would just wait out the process.

In a culture where so much focus is on quick results, we tend to bypass process. I'm not naturally pre-dispositioned to focus on process. For me, it takes deliberate, intentional effort to process or to wait. I'm learning, though, as I wait and as I allow process to take place, all areas of my life are like the brisket – flavorful and tender.

God created the whole world and didn't need a to-do list. He just spoke and *poof* there it was. The details are nothing for Him. He is working all things out. You may not see it but He does. He sees all things. He is the I AM.

In the middle of crisis, waiting is particularly difficult. We may ask God what to do but when we are face-to-face with a deadline, we often jump to make a decision instead of waiting on God to answer. In the middle of crisis, life is often cloudy and full of confusion. God brings clarity. He is not about confusing us. When I feel confused, I have to talk to God and allow Him to remove the confusion and replace it with clarity. I find clarity in being still before God. Clearing my mind and letting Him speak to me.

In his lecture in New York in 1869, James Smith says:[v]

> But however discouraging your circumstances may be, however dull and dreary you may be in your soul, or cast down on account of the difficulties of the way, still wait on the Lord, nor shall you wait in vain.
>
> Difficulties often arise from our ignorance, or relations in life, or the duties that devolve upon us. These difficulties are often great, so that we know not what to do, or which way to take. Our wisdom is swallowed up, and our friends are unable to advise us. One rash step may ruin us. We appear to be impelled and urged to go forward, and yet are afraid to take a step. Every plan we have formed has failed; every effort has been abortive. We dare not go back;

we fear to go forward– and yet we feel as if we could not stand still. We imagine that no creature was ever tried as we are. We have been sincere, and yet have gone wrong. We have tried our best, and yet have failed. We are tempted to envy others who succeed, to think that the Lord has dealt harshly with us, and even to become reckless. Before us are difficulties, seemingly as great as the Red Sea before Israel; behind us are obstacles, as fearful as the Egyptians behind them. Besides which, we have no Moses with the rod of God to make a way for us.

What can we do? Do as the prophet of old did, who said– "I will wait upon the Lord, who hides his face from the house of Jacob, and I will look for him." Yes, wait on the Lord, who has given you this precious promise– "I will instruct you and teach you in the way which you shall go; I will guide you with my eye." He will point out the way, he will teach you in the way, he will guide as a loving Father or a faithful friend. There are no difficulties with him. He sees the end from the beginning. He has directed thousands, millions, who have been in as great or greater difficulties than you are. What he has done for others, he will do for you. Hear his own word– "I will bring the blind by a way that they knew not; I will lead them in paths that they have not known; I will make darkness light before them, and crooked things straight. These things will I do unto them, and not forsake them." Wait, therefore, on the Lord, and say– "Behold, as the eyes of servants look unto the hand of their masters, and as the eyes of a maiden unto the hand of her mistress; so our eyes wait upon the Lord our God, until that he have mercy upon us."

When I was a kid, we would have family devotions. Sometimes we would each read our favorite scripture. Psalm 27 was always my favorite scripture as a kid. It seems I always focused on the 'you don't have to be afraid' part of this Psalm. I was afraid a lot and worried a lot as a kid. Psalm 27 gave me courage. But this Psalm is so much more.

1 The Lord is my light and my salvation— whom shall I fear? The Lord is the stronghold of my life— of whom shall I be afraid? 2 When evil men advance against me to devour my flesh, when my enemies and my foes attack me, they will stumble and fall. 3 Though an army besiege me, my heart will not fear; though war break out against me, even then will I be confident. 4 One thing I ask of the Lord, this is what I seek: that I may dwell in the house of the Lord all the days of my life, to gaze upon the beauty of the Lord and to seek him in his temple. 5 For in the day of trouble he will keep me safe in his dwelling; he will hide me in the shelter of his tabernacle and set me high upon a rock. 6 Then my head will be exalted above the enemies who surround me; at his tabernacle will I sacrifice with shouts of joy; I will sing and make music to the Lord.

7 Hear my voice when I call, O Lord; be merciful to me and answer me. 8 My heart says of you, "Seek his face!" Your face, Lord, I will seek. 9 Do not hide your face from me, do not turn your servant away in anger; you have been my helper. Do not reject me or forsake me, O God my Savior. 10 Though my father and mother forsake me, the Lord will receive me. 11 Teach me your way, O Lord; lead me in a straight path because of my oppressors. 12 Do not turn me over to the desire of my foes, for false witnesses rise up against me, breathing out violence. 13 I am still confident of this: I will see the goodness of the Lord in the land of the living. 14 Wait for the Lord; be strong and take heart and wait for the Lord.

I think it is beautiful how David moves through this Psalm. He begins with identifying who God is - my light, my salvation, stronghold of my life. Because of who God is, David has no reason to fear. He has confidence even when he is attacked or is besieged by an army. David knows about God's might and power from experience. He then has a request. It's not to be free from battles or to crush his enemy. It is to dwell in the house of the Lord and gaze upon the beauty of the Lord. He pledges to seek God's face. He implores God to not forsake him. David asks God to teach him and lead him. Then he ends with "wait for the Lord." But, it is not just wait; it is be strong, take heart and wait. This is a waiting full of hope and expectation. It is waiting knowing God's going to do something. The Hebrew word for wait is qavah. It means to wait, look for, hope, expect; look eagerly for; to linger for.[vi] This is an active waiting. It is not just going about life forgetting what we're waiting for, swallowed up by daily activity. It is not sitting in the dark with covers over our head in despair. It is actively hoping, expecting, listening and lingering for God. Wait.

Waiting like 'qavah' waiting involves a clear understanding of who God is. If we don't know God, if we are unfamiliar with God's character, then, we can't wait with expectation. When we know who God is, we are compelled to wait on Him.

Have you ever had to wait on someone? I have too many times. Usually it is extremely frustrating for me, especially if I feel pressured for a deadline. There were many occasions as a consultant where I had to wait on people to give me information so I could complete a project. It seemed like the bigger the project the later people would get information to me. Then, I would have to cram forty hours of work into 16 hours. That kind of waiting was frustrating.

When we were dating, Jimmy would frequently be late. We would have a time set to meet on campus. I would get there and wait. Sometimes I would wait for over an hour. I was afraid to leave, because I didn't want to not be there when he showed up. So, I waited. At times I would be upset, disappointed or hurt because he forgot or just got busy and left me waiting. But, the waiting was always worthwhile because the reward was spending time with my favorite person.

In early 2005, the pastor of a church near Suva, Fiji became frustrated with the slow progress of his new church building. The three year old construction consisted of a building frame. He purchased building supplies as the church could afford them. Some weeks it was only one board and other weeks it was nothing. So, Pastor Moses decided to write a letter to some other churches in Fiji to ask for help. As he wrote the letter, he felt he should address it to God instead of the churches. He placed the letter in his Bible, telling no one.

In the meantime, we had a friend in Kansas who watched a show about Fiji on TV. While watching the show, he felt God wanted to do work somewhere in Fiji. After some research, he located a missionary in Fiji and made contact. Before the contact came, the missionary had driven by the slowly developing building for years. The missionary did not know the pastor but felt like someone needed to help with the building. We were part of the team that worked on Pastor Moses' church. Within one week, we were able to build the walls, roof, floor and the team gave enough funds to purchase the paint for the building.

Pastor Moses waited and put His complete trust in God. God did not fail. He put all the pieces of the puzzle together. He read the letter; He called a team; He directed a missionary.

Jesus' first recorded miracle is turning the water into wine. We read the account and it is really cool to see Jesus' creativity in the miracle and His power. The thing that stands out to me, though, is the response of the master. He is shocked the wine at the end of the feast was better than the wine at the beginning. (John 2:10) What Jesus does is always the best. Our greatest efforts pale in comparison to what He does. The whole water to wine miracle was a spur of the moment solution to a problem. Jesus didn't have a four step plan prepared three weeks ahead of time. He didn't have to sit down with his committee of disciples to figure out how to handle the situation. Guess what – He hasn't changed a bit since then. Sometimes the answer doesn't appear to us as quickly as the wine did but when Jesus answers we can expect the very best.

As we wait for God's provision and direction, we are often tempted to take control ourselves. If we give in to the lure of control, we will undoubtedly miss out on God's greater blessing. I am full of confidence in who God is and what He is capable of. He is the creator; He is the Lord of Heaven's Armies; He is Jehovah; He is my Banner; He is my Provider; He is I AM! He is worth waiting for every time.

Chapter 6 – Relationships

Exodus 17:12 When Moses' hands grew tired, they took a stone and put it under him and he sat on it. Aaron and Hur held his hands up—one on one side, one on the other—so that his hands remained steady till sunset.

We build walls for churches, shelters and schools. Walls are not designed to exist around our hearts. From the third grade throughout high school, I constructed a spectacular structure around my heart. My objective was self-preservation. I didn't want to be made fun of anymore. I didn't want to be hurt again. I convinced myself I didn't need friends. Deep inside I had a craving to have a friend but I suppressed the feeling because I was afraid. I adapted the motto that I was just fine on my own. I spent time with mom and dad's friends and other adults at church. I had some very shallow friendships. I didn't let anyone past the fortress to my heart.

I gradually … very gradually … started allowing people to be friends in college. Just a couple of months into my freshman year of college, I met Jimmy. Wow! I was smitten with his striking blue eyes, his dynamic personality and his smile. He made my heart melt. When we started dating, I was consumed by fear he would not like me. The words I said most to him for the first year we dated were "I'm sorry." I apologized for everything to the point he would get mad at me for apologizing so much. We had a lot of fun together. Yet, I was still afraid if I didn't do what he wanted, when he wanted it and how he wanted it he would walk away from me. I truly could not believe he wanted to be with me. We've been married for almost twenty years. I'm not afraid any more.

My college years were very therapeutic and healing for me. The fortress crumbled floor by floor until there was only a small fence remaining. The fence survived for a few more years. After my 2004 trip to Jamaica, the fence was burned down and my heart now is completely exposed and happily so. Now, I don't know how I could survive without my friends. There is unbelievable power & support in the company of friends, especially friends who serve God. Not all of my friends live near me. In fact, my dearest friend lives several hours away. But her support, prayers and friendship have made a huge impact on my life.

I used to read Exodus 17:12 and wondered if I would ever have someone like Aaron and Hur to stand with me. Since then, God has blessed me with several dear friends who do stand with me in a variety of ways. God has created us to have relationships and to stand with each other.

I'm at a point in my life where I need deeper relationships. I want and need those relationships that are completely open and transparent, that are deep and challenging. I've had enough shallow, surface level relationships. I know not every relationship will be deep. I have several relationships that are fun and great for a good time but are truly rather shallow. My heart really desires the refreshing, challenging, accountability and openness found in deep relationships.

There is comfort in having friends you can be totally open with and who do the same in return. Nothing hidden.

No underlying agendas. Complete transparency. Not every friend is this way. There are four different levels of friendship.

The first level of friendship is "Familiars." This group of friends can be quite large. I have over 300 Facebook friends. Most of these friends are Familiars. We don't really know these friends all that well. We greet, smile at and talk briefly with Familiars. Familiars converse about general issues like the weather, current events or work. There is not a strong connection with Familiars but they are great for networking. You infrequently visit or communicate with Familiars. There is a low emotional tie. The friendship is not usually a long-term friendship. It may be an old friend who has lost touch, such as a high school friend or previous co-worker. When they ask how you are, you say fine whether you are or not. These are the people you may say hello to if you see them at the restaurant but you will likely not go out of your way to talk to them. Familiars will never see you without your make-up on or hair done.

The second level of friendship is "Buddies." This group of friends is significantly smaller than Familiars, usually around 20-30 people. These may be considered good friends but lack a deep level of intimacy or have a low frequency of contact. Buddies may be friends who live in different cities, siblings, neighbors or may be in a small group with you. At the Buddies level, friendship is based on common interests and activities. We know these friends better than at the Familiars level. Buddies share ideas and problems in a general way at the surface level. When they ask how are you, you may tell the truth but in a vague or general way. If you are going through a rough time, you may say so but not elaborate on the details. You might meet Buddies somewhere for lunch or have them over to your house and treat them as special guests.

The third level of friendship is "Comrades" This group of friends is even smaller than Buddies – usually 10-12 people. You spend time with them and have common values. You talk about deep things, such as plans, problems and goals with your Comrades. These friends are great accountability partners. You know these friends well. Jesus' twelve disciples were Comrades. He shared meals with them and spent quality time with them talking about important things. He shared experiences with them and helped them grow. When a Comrade asks how you are, you tell them the truth with detail about some areas of your life. You still protect some things. You have Comrades over for dinner and they make themselves at home. These are the friends who I have the most fun with. If you have good news to celebrate or tragedy to grieve over, you want your Comrades to know about it.

The fourth level of friendship is "Confidants." These are the closest friends. This is a very small group - usually just one to three people. There is a strong intimacy in these relationships. Friendship with confidants is based on a commitment, transparency and availability to one another. Confidants develop the potential of each other. They share the deepest and most personal information. Jesus' Confidants were Peter, James, and John. Confidants are with us in our most glorious and our most horrific moments. These friends will challenge us, inspire us and grow with us. Confidants are the friends you would take a bullet for. When they ask how you are, you tell them the truth with detail and they help you cope. These friends not only see you without your make-up on, they will sit with you and hold your hand as you face life's most difficult moments.

The Bible has many examples of friendships. While the Bible doesn't expound on the relationship between Shadrach, Meshach and Abednego, I can just imagine they were the closest of Confidants. Look at all they went through together. Shadrach, Meshach, and Abednego were essentially hostages taken to Babylon. (Daniel 1-3) They were young nobility and very intelligent. Along with Daniel, they refused to abandon their beliefs in God, which bound them together. They were promoted in their jobs in Babylon. Shadrach, Meshach and Abednego are most famous for their trip into the fiery furnace. King Nebuchadnezzar signed a new law stating anyone who doesn't bow down and worship his big statue when certain music plays will be thrown in the fiery furnace. So, the new law is communicated to the people. Shadrach, Meshach and Abednego refuse to bow down and worship anything but God. Neb's crew is watching the three Hebrew young men and notice they are disobeying the law. Shadrach, Meshach and Abednego declare their firm belief in God's ability to save them. Neb tells the furnace workers to heat the furnace seven times hotter than usual. He was furious. Then the soldiers throw Shadrach, Meshach and Abednego into the furnace. The furnace was so hot, the soldiers were killed. While the boys are in the furnace, a fourth man shows up – a man who looks like the son of God. Not a hair on their heads was singed. Even their clothes were unharmed by the flames. Can you imagine what was going through Meshach's mind as he looked at Abednego and Shadrach? What do you think Abednego told his grandchildren about his time in the furnace? I believe their shared experience in the fiery furnace was a regular conversation piece at family get-togethers. These friends experienced successes together and experienced tremendous trials together. I can imagine them sitting together encouraging one another – 'we can make it' – congratulating each other – 'I'm so happy for you' – praying together. In short, they experienced life together. Sharing life experiences is what friends do.

I've often thought we should have an interview process to determine if someone qualifies to be one of our Buddies or Comrades and most certainly our Confidants. My closest friends must be divinely appointed because I don't know any other way we would have met or bonded. God has placed us in the right place at the right time to meet each other. Some friends have only been in my life for a season, others for a few seasons. While an interview process would select friends who meet our own idea of the friend we need, those God places in our lives are uniquely qualified to fill a gap we may not even see.

My first best friend was in my life for a time when I needed to learn about friendship. I had friends who were Familiars and some Buddies but at that point in my life I didn't have any Comrades and my only Confidant was Jimmy. She helped me open up and had a huge impact on the kind of friend I am today. We connected the first time we met. It seemed like we had known each other our entire life. I never thought I would have a best friend like her.

Although God blessed me with several friends on all levels, I have experienced a separation from many of them as we are doing the work of Clear Vision Ministries. The more we do for God and the more we work at fulfilling His plan for our lives, the more we are attacked. A lot of people don't want to be around when times are tough. Relationships are important but the right relationships are essential. Our time and energy needs to focus on the right relationships and disengage from distracting or unhealthy relationships.

~ Unhealthy Relationships ~

Have you ever been around someone who just absolutely sucks the energy out of you – kind of like an energy leech? Maybe it's the friend who is always negative. You know the type who finds something wrong in everything. Or, it could be the friend who is the victim. Everyone is out to get her. There's also the intimidator. This is the person who builds herself up by putting everyone else down. Unhealthy relationships are those that leave you feeling energy drained, hurt, inadequate or put down. I'm not talking about a one-time occurrence of any of these traits. Unhealthy relationships have one or more of these or other unhealthy traits on an ongoing basis.

If you are in an unhealthy relationship, the first question to ask yourself is if the relationship is salvageable. I am not talking about your desire to salvage the relationship. I'm talking about if the relationship has potential to be healthy. If so, then, you need to talk to the other person in a constructive manner. Prepare before the conversation. Think about what you need to say and how you are going to say it. Be specific in your communication. If you really want to salvage the relationship, you cannot be vague when describing the issues. Write down some examples of the behaviors causing the unhealthiness in the relationship. Writing out your key points will help you stay on track and will help you to not miss any key issues. When you have the conversation, control your emotions. Be calm and sincere. One of the best methods to communicate a tough message with someone is called an "I statement". "I statements" focus on the results of the person's behavior rather than on the person. It also communicates a problem to another person without accusing them of being the cause of the problem. Below is an "I Statement" Formula. I have used this formula in numerous training, coaching and disciplinary settings, as well as in my own relationships.

When I (saw, heard, etc.)

I felt (what emotion you felt)

Because I (what interpretations support those feelings)

Pause (let the other person respond)

And now I would like (what action, information or commitment do you want now)

So that (what positive results will that action lead to)

What do you think? (listen to what the other person says – are they willing to do what is needed to make the relationship work or resolve the issue)

For example: **When I heard** you say that I am about as close to being a genius as the rock in our front yard, **I felt** embarrassed and humiliated **because I** have worked hard to learn and improve my skills. (**pause**) **I would like** for you to not put me down or make fun of me **so that** I can talk to you without feeling hurt. **What do you think**?

"I statements" are not easy at first. As with all learning, it takes practice to become comfortable with the process. Ask a trustworthy friend to practice with you. If the relationship is worth saving, then, fight past the urge to give up rather than prepare and practice for the conversation. You should also be prepared to hear the other person refute what you say and even tell you things you are doing that hurt the relationship. Most likely your friend will not follow the tips outlined here. The worst response you can have is to become defensive. If you become defensive, your friend will mirror you and also become defensive and you will not accomplish anything.

After the initial conversation, create a plan of action with your friend. What are each of you going to do to make the relationship work? How will you communicate with each other when one of you does something that makes the relationship unhealthy?

If you have determined the relationship is not salvageable, you should still communicate the message to your friend unless you feel it is too unsafe for you to do so. After you have told the other person how you feel, honestly and tactfully tell them that you believe the relationship is not healthy for you and you need to remove yourself from the relationship. Again, you are stating what you feel and what you need to do rather than blaming the other person.

~ Accountability Partner ~

Having an accountability partner is honestly not something I ever thought about until four or five years ago. I had never even heard anyone talk about accountability partners in the church world. As a 'use what you learn' tool, I regularly asked my training participants and coaching clients to set up accountability partnerships. But, I never thought about accountability partnerships with friends or church family.

> *Galatians 6:1-2 Brothers, if someone is caught in a sin, you who are spiritual should restore him gently. But watch yourself, or you also may be tempted. Carry each other's burdens, and in this way you will fulfill the law of Christ.*

> *James 5:16 Therefore confess your sins to each other and pray for each other so that you may be healed. The prayer of a righteous man is powerful and effective.*

> *1 Thessalonians 5:11 Therefore encourage one another and build each other up, just as in fact you are doing.*

An accountability partner is someone you can confide in and be completely transparent with. She is someone you completely trust. Accountability partners share life experiences and pray with each other. Accountability partners build each other up and encourage spiritual growth. Accountability partners ask the hard questions and are trustworthy enough to hear the whole truth.

I have found accountability partnerships to be incredibly rewarding. When you converse with someone on a deep level, you experience a real connection. For an accountability partnership to have the greatest impact and effectiveness, create an agreement listing roles, responsibilities and ground rules for the relationship. While this may seem a little overboard, you want to make sure both individuals have the same understanding of the nature of the relationship and expectations of confidentiality, encouragement and prayer. The agreement does not have to be in writing as long as both individuals clearly understand what is expected in the relationship. I have engaged in accountability partnerships without discussing expectations and roles. I ended up feeling frustrated because I asked the hard questions and got fluff answers. I felt like I was trying to go deep in the relationship and help my friend grow and I was getting nothing in return. Accountability partnerships are truly a partnership – it is not a one-sided deal.

As part of the agreement, identify how frequently you will meet and communicate with each other. My personal preference is meeting face-to-face monthly and communicating by phone or email at least weekly – especially if my partner is going through a tough time. Below are some sample questions you can discuss with an accountability partner. These are just suggestions. Sit down with your partner and create a list of questions you will regularly ask each other.

1. What is going good in your life right now?
2. What challenges are you facing?
3. Tell me about your personal time with the Lord this week.
4. How is your relationship with Jesus?
5. How have you been tempted this week? How did you respond?
6. Did you worship in church this week?
7. Have you heard God's heart beat this week?
8. What is God speaking to you?
9. How are things with your spouse? (time together, spiritual life, etc.)
10. How are things going with your kids? (time together, spiritual life, etc.)
11. How is your job?
12. How is your balance of work and family?
13. How well are you living by your priorities?
14. Are you where you feel God wants you to be right now?
15. What thoughts are you having that are not healthy?
16. How have you positively impacted others this week?

~ In the Absence of Present Friends ~

I often find myself relying on the Lord's presence in the absence of present friends. Being present is more than a physical location. Have you ever been in the middle of a conversation and thought you might as well be talking to a rock? The person you are talking to may be physically near you but she is not really present. Presence is a mental and emotional connectedness that defies physical proximity. It is listening on the edge of our seats, completely focused and demonstrating we are paying attention. We've probably all been absent a few times when we should have been present with our friends. I know I have. I've half listened while thinking about other things. I've listened but spent my mental energy placing judgment instead of demonstrating understanding. I've also been on the receiving end of an absent friend. I've listened to responses that sounded like pre-recorded answers instead of authentic response.

I recently watched an episode of One Tree Hill[vii]. In this episode, Sam, who is a teenage foster kid, is saying good-bye to her best friend. Jack, too, is a foster child and had just found a family to live with in another city. They say good-bye and Jack gets in the car to leave with his new family. Then the screen shows Sam standing by herself on the side-walk with tears streaming down her face. She reaches both hands around behind her and holds her own hand. I know it is just a TV show but I seriously cried here. Sam felt alone. There was no one present for her at this moment. Have you ever been in a similar place? I have. Maybe the reason I relate emotionally to Sam's scene is because I've been left standing alone with no one to hold my hand. In those times my heart literally aches to have physical contact with a friend who is present. There is good news. Even though I would really enjoy a 'present' friend, I have a friend named Jesus who is always, always with me. I know He is truly my very best friend, my most intimate friend. When no one else is present to hold my hand, He is holding it. You may be sitting in the absence of present friends, either because of proximity or connectedness but you are not alone. Jesus is with you and He is the best friend you can ever have.

As I'm sitting here freezing, with two blankets, a sweater and heating pad, I can't help but think how cold life would be on the inside without God and the people He puts in our lives. Cold on the outside is uncomfortable. I can't stand being cold. I'm tired of winter after the first five minutes. But, it is only a level of comfortableness. Inside in my heart and mind I am warm. I am warmed by the Lord's presence, by His love, by His friendship. I cannot imagine what life would be like without my Lord – cold, empty, uncertain. Even in the midst of trials that seem unbearable, God's presence is soothing, comforting...warming. On top of that, God blesses us with people He has strategically and divinely placed in our lives. Those relationships, the conversations, the prayers, the hugs, the like-mindedness, the encouragement inspire us, stretch us, build us up, unite us, join the battle with us, spur us on, warm us. So, as I sit here freezing on the outside, I am warm and toasty on the inside.

Chapter 7 – Finding My Voice

Exodus 4: 12 Now go! I will be with you as you speak, and I will instruct you in what to say.

I almost always have something to say. In fact, it is rare for me to be speechless. Wisdom is knowing when and how to deliver the message so it has maximum impact in the most effective manner. Boldness is having the guts to say what needs to be said even if it is difficult.

It took me a long time to be bold enough to share my voice. I always had thoughts, ideas, and opinions – but was too afraid to share it because of what others might say. I am so glad I found my voice. Now, I pray for wisdom in using that voice.

I'm inspired every time we go to another country to work. In no place do the voices, the boldness, the passion and commitment stand out to me like they do in China. Courage and commitment. I read and hear the term 'believer' quite often. I compare the American Christian to the Chinese Christian or the Romanian Christian and I wonder how much of a true believer we are. Are we willing to risk everything for what we believe? Would you risk being alienated from your family for Christ or risk being tortured or imprisoned? Do we speak and share what we have to say about what we believe or do we stay silent or dilute it so much there is no significance.

Words are powerful. God spoke the world into existence. Jesus spoke peace and the storms became still. Words can heal; words can destroy. In Matthew 17:20, Jesus tells the disciples if they have just a little bit of faith they can tell a mountain to move and it will be moved. Do you understand what this means? With a word, we can move mountains if we have faith. Mountains will move by the power of God in us as we speak out in faith – using our voice.

> *"...not that it would be ordinarily or ever done in a literal sense by the apostles, that they should remove mountains; but that they should be able to do things equally difficult, and as seemingly impossible, if they had but faith, when the glory of God, and the good of men, required it."*[viii]

Our voice is more than the sound we make when we open our mouth. It represents the verbal and non-verbal expression of our values. When we place value on something, we talk about it, protect it, promote it and take risks for it. We also position ourselves to prohibit influences opposing what we value.

We were visiting my parents and I noticed there was a clock in every room. Most of the clocks were making the ticking sound for each passing second. I started thinking about the importance of time and the variety of reasons people have time priorities. Is the time important so we can get one more task done, so we wonder how much longer? So we think about what we should have done. But what about asking if we have spent our time on what we value. I think this is a valid question to ask. Why the clocks? Are we rushing the wrong things because of numbers on a ticking device? Do we spend our precious moments on things that matter? I know I don't always spend my time wisely and sometimes I do rush good things for the sake of those blasted numbers. God help me to be more aware and more determined to spend my time wisely. Maybe life is better when we don't have the clock and we linger on good things until God is really ready for us to move on. How we spend our time is a non-verbal expression of our values.

In many of the countries we have visited, time is not really all that important. I remember one missionary telling us church starts at 6:00 pm. At 6:30 pm, he then said we didn't need to leave the house to get to church for another thirty minutes. So, we waited. When we arrived, church hadn't started yet. Most everyone was still in the process of arriving. The church service began around 7:00 pm. No one was rushed leaving either. People stayed around to pray and talk to other people. When I left, I had no idea we had been there for almost four hours. Time – the numbers on the clock – didn't matter, but the lingering on the good things was priceless.

I understand we cannot just show up to work whenever we feel like it and spend all day on one task we feel is important at the expense of other critical tasks. I've facilitated more time management and life balance trainings than I can count. Businesses are interested in time management so employees can be more productive and stop wasting time. People, in general, are interested in life balance so they can get the most out of their time at work, home and wherever else they want to spend time. Time is a precious limited commodity. There is absolutely nothing you can do to gain more time. All you can do is use the time wisely. For me, this means focusing on the things that matter most to me – my personal relationship with God, my family, our ministry, my own personal well-being and my friends.

I want my friends and family to be healthy, successful and happy. I want deep relationships with my friends. I want Taylor to be a mighty man of God. I want Jimmy to have his hearts desires and to be a spiritual warrior son of the Almighty. I want to feel good. I want to be able to do everything Clear Vision Ministries is meant to do with no financial restrictions. I want to go wherever God opens doors and see miracles take place. These values and priorities drive me to action.

Why do we do what we do? Part of the answer for me is found in Zephaniah 3:9-13 and 17.

> *9"For at that time I will change the speech of the peoples to a pure speech, that all of them may call upon the name of the LORD and serve him with one accord. 10 From beyond the rivers of Cush my worshipers, the daughter of my dispersed ones, shall bring my offering. 11 "On that day you shall not be put to shame because of the deeds by which you have rebelled against me; for then I will remove from your midst your proudly exultant ones, and you shall no longer be haughty in my holy mountain. 12But I will leave in your midst a people humble and lowly. They shall seek refuge in the name of the LORD, 13 those who are left in Israel; they shall do no injustice and speak no lies, nor shall there be found in their mouth a deceitful tongue. For they shall graze and lie down, and none shall make them afraid."*

> *17 The LORD your God is in your midst, a mighty one who will save; he will rejoice over you with gladness; he will quiet you by his love; he will exult over you with loud singing.*

We play a small part in changing lives so that **all** will call upon the name of the LORD and serve him. Christ followers are responsible for telling others about Him. God's desire is for everyone to call on Him and serve Him every day wherever they are. When we call on Him, serve Him, worship Him and seek refuge in Him, then, we can graze and lie down and nothing will make us afraid. He delights in me. He delights in you.

When I am doing the work God has called me to do, my heart feels so full. God is enough to fill every space in our heart, mind and life. He is enough to sustain us and fulfill us. There is nothing greater in life than an intimate relationship with God.

In verse 17, Zephaniah says God is in our midst. He is with us right where we are. He rejoices over us. He exults over us. To exult means, "to show or feel a lively or triumphant joy; rejoice exceedingly; be highly elated or jubilant."[ix] My mind struggles to comprehend how God Almighty rejoices over us. The concept is as dichotomous as a beggar living in a multi-billion dollar mansion. God rejoices over us similarly to how we rejoice over our children, just multiplied to the nth degree. When Taylor preached his first sermon, I was highly elated. When he describes how helping others makes him feel, I rejoice exceedingly (and I cry a little, too). When he makes straight A's in classes a grade-level or two above where he should be, I am jubilant. I am proud of him – of what he does and who he is. I AM exults over us! Wow! I am swept away by this personal attention from God.

When we went to Romania, we visited a very poor village church. When we left, Taylor said, "They have so little, but they have given so much." This has been true in every country we have been. The people seem to find 'enough' in God rather than stuff. God really is enough. In our life, we have experienced God as 'enough' over and over. God is really all we need. In the USA we tend to always want more – of everything: clothes, food, money, space, time, comfort, etc. It seems like we are a very self-focused and stuff-focused group of people. We never have enough.

As I seek to hear and live in sync with God's heartbeat, I am overwhelmed. I wish I was an artist so I could paint how I feel. As I think about His goodness, grace, love and mercy, I can hardly breathe. I ache to be in His very throne room. I know He is always with me but I want so much to be in His throne room. At the same time, I think about all of the people we've met in Romania, China, Honduras, Mexico, Ecuador and Fiji. There are so many people around the world who don't know God, who desperately need Him. The agony I feel within me isn't for the pain in my body, though it is real. Nor is it for the bills we can't pay, though there are many. The agony I feel is for the need in the hearts of men, women and children around the world who need God's love and for the missionaries who are struggling and need encouragement. We need Jehovah Jireh to help us and to let His light shine on us and through us. I can't imagine how God's heart aches. I have such a limited understanding and visibility of the world's population compared to God's view. But, just the glimpse I see makes my heart hurt so deeply. We have to look beyond ourselves to see the world. We need to look at the scope of things outside our immediate bubble. I want to live my life everyday with a proximity so near to God I can hear His heart beating. I want to be close enough I can sense His agony, joy and compassion. This is the focus of my voice.

Every one of us will leave a legacy of some kind. She was a great friend and mother. He was a successful businessman. She was the smartest person. He accumulated wealth. She helped a lot of people. What will I be known as? What quality or characteristic will people see in me? I hope my legacy shows Jesus living in and through me; that I was a difference maker; that I was a faithful friend; that I fulfilled everything God had planned for me to do.

In the previous chapter, we looked at relationships. One of the keys to building those relationships is effective communication. I've done a ton of communication skills training in my career as a consultant. Having good communication really boils down to being present in the conversation, listening intently, adapting to the behavioral style of the other person and clearly voicing your message in a way the receiver can understand. There are a lot of different reasons communication breaks down – not paying attention, attitude towards the other person or subject matter, distractions, busyness, etc. I think one of the biggest break downs in communication among those we are the closest to happens because we know the person so well we assume they will know what we are talking about. So, we become cryptic, miss key points and rarely check to make sure the other person really understands what we are saying. I think we often try harder with communicating to someone we don't know than those we are close to. We are more intentional in conversations with people we don't know as well. We give more detail and specifics because we don't know what the other person knows. It's easy to ask your spouse a question and while he's answering be watching TV or reading or playing with the kids or doing housework. Or, as you are telling him something, you use vague words (it, they, some, etc.) and expect him to read your mind for the details.

Being present in the conversation involves removing distractions and placing our complete attention on the person we are speaking with. We pay attention to what is said and how it is said. We let the other person know we are present by giving non-verbal cues, such as eye contact, nodding our head in understanding, smiling, leaning forward and verbal cues. We stop multi-tasking during conversations. I can't stand talking to someone who is not present in the conversation. It's like telling the person they are not worth full attention or they are too busy to devote the time for conversation. When you are present in the conversation, you convey to the other person how important they are and how invested you are in the conversation.

Listening intently entails listening to the words said, the intended meaning of what is said and the emotions behind what it said. As we listen intently, we can identify variances in the words spoken and the emotion behind them. For example, if you ask a friend if they are ok and the words spoken are 'I'm fine' but you see remnants of tears in her eyes, there is variance. Listening intently also includes organizing the information in a way to see the big picture of what the speaker is saying. One of my friends likes to give a tremendous amount of detail as she tells a story. Oftentimes, she strays away from the main thing she is telling me. So, as I listen intently to her, I sort the information into categories relevant, non-relevant and may be relevant. By doing this, I can critically think about what she is saying and truly understand the point of the conversation. Listening is more than just hearing; it is really about understanding.

Adapting to the behavioral style of the other person you are communicating with is actually a powerful communication tool. There are four basic behavioral styles. Each of us have a combination of the four primary styles in our individual behavior.[x]

Dominant	**Influence**
• Results focused • Direct • Loves challenge • Sees the big picture • Competitive • Fast paced	• People focused • Optimistic • Unorganized • Outgoing • Animated • Fast paced
Steadiness	**Conscientiousness**
• Cooperates with others • Predictable • Values stability • Fears change • Calm • Slow paced	• Focuses on quality • Task oriented • Analytical • Tends to be perfectionists • Cautious • Slow paced

Adapting based on the behavioral style of the person you are talking to allows the other person to feel more comfortable with the communication. The key really is making the conversation about the other person's comfort instead of our own. If you are talking to someone who is primarily Dominant, you would not communicate the details as much as you would for a primary Conscientiousness. I am a Dominant/Influence style, so I want the big picture and I want it fast. I want to see results but I also really care about the relationship. When I talk to someone who is Steadiness or Conscientiousness, I have to slow my pace and allow them to communicate the details in their own time. Adapting is not easy at first but with practice it becomes second nature.

Clearly voicing your message in a way the receiver can understand begins with using language the receiver understands. For non-medically trained people, technical doctor-speak and terminology can be confusing. If you've ever watched a medical television show, you hear words like ten-blade, thoracotomy tray, cyanotic, etc. This is almost like a foreign language. Use terminology the other person will understand. That does not mean you need to dumb-down what you are saying. Instead, you describe in enough detail for difficult concepts to be understood. Clearly voicing your message also includes being specific in what you say and describing what you are saying so the listener can picture it as you intend it.

Communicating effectively is essential in using our voice. How we say what we value often dictates how people will receive what we say. If we are wishy-washy or do not display confidence, others will see what we say as insignificant. If we are pushy and confrontational, others will see us as a bully and discount what we say.

Your desired legacy, relationships and communication work together in developing your voice. Begin working on communicating your purpose to those around you in how you live, what you do, what you say and how you respond to life. Let your voice ring out.

Chapter 8 – It's Okay to Rest

1 Kings 19:3 Elijah was afraid and ran for his life. When he came to Beersheba in Judah, he left his servant there, 4 while he himself went a day's journey into the desert. He came to a broom tree, sat down under it and prayed that he might die. "I have had enough, Lord," he said. "Take my life; I am no better than my ancestors." 5 Then he lay down under the tree and fell asleep. All at once an angel touched him and said, "Get up and eat." 6 He looked around, and there by his head was a cake of bread baked over hot coals, and a jar of water. He ate and drank and then lay down again. 7 The angel of the Lord came back a second time and touched him and said, "Get up and eat, for the journey is too much for you." 8 So he got up and ate and drank. Strengthened by that food, he traveled forty days and forty nights until he reached Horeb, the mountain of God.

~ Perspective ~

When Elijah, the prophet of God, fled, he was in total despair and praying to die. Then in verses 5-6, he fell asleep. The angel woke him up so he could eat and drink.

He needed physical rest, food and drink - he was exhausted. As I reflect, his perspective was altered by his physical well-being. He was ready to give up. If you look at verse 8, after he was strengthened, he traveled 40 days to get to Mt. Horeb. There have been a lot of days when I have been in so much pain I prayed or wished God would just let me die. There are also a lot of days where I don't feel like - or even want to - do anything because I am so exhausted and hurting so much. My perspective has been totally shifted on those days because of my physical exhaustion.

Think about this concept in a big picture. I know a lot of people who have autoimmune disease, like RA, of some sort. We are all exhausted and in pain. There are a lot of people who are completely controlled by disease (or other life circumstance). They are limited in what they are able to do in life. I know I do so much less than I could if I felt well. It seems like there is a whole generation of women who are suffering. Think about how many people you know – especially women – who suffer from chronic pain, chronic fatigue syndrome, fibromyalgia, autoimmune diseases or other life altering chronic conditions. How many do you know? At least one-third of the women I know suffer from one or more of these conditions. As a result of this epidemic, I wonder how much of God's work is not being done. While I understand the true physical nature of these conditions on an all too personal level, I also believe there is a pretty intense spiritual battle going on for the fitness of God's children. If Elijah would not have had the physical rest and nourishment, he would not have made it to the rest of his story. With that said, we all really need physical rest and nourishment, just like Elijah - not just to help us with our perspective but to also allow us to completely fulfill God's plan for our lives. Even if God does not heal us or change our circumstance, He can still give us rest. I've come to rely on the rest from

God. Not so much a physical rest but a peace and strength in spite of how I feel kind of rest.

You may not be suffering from a disease or physical condition but I dare say everyone has experienced some form of exhaustion. Maybe you work twelve hours a day, six days a week or maybe you are a single parent, working hard, taking care of the kids, the house and everyone but yourself or maybe your parents are elderly and you are now responsible for their care in addition to your spouse and children. Whatever the cause, I cannot think of a single person who has not experienced some form of exhaustion.

Exhaustion has an interesting affect on people. When we're exhausted, everything impacts us in a bigger way. I'm more prone to get sick when I'm exhausted. I'm also more likely to cry, get irritated and my pain level goes up. It makes an interesting mix!

What are we supposed to do when we feel this way? I have tried to copy Elijah's experience. God hasn't sent an angel or miraculously made food appear but he rested, received nourishment, talked to God and got some perspective. For a long time, I could not allow myself to rest. There was always too much to get done. Too many other priorities. Too many undone tasks. Too much worry about what others would think. It makes sense, though, that we need rest. We need nourishment. We need to talk to God. We need some perspective. Without these things, we will find ourselves in the same boat as Elijah and be ready for God to just let us die. I've been there more times than I would like to admit. But now I know there is hope. I was familiar with the concept of rest before but now I have experienced it and really know it.

Taking advantage of God's rest doesn't mean I can be reckless and get away with it. I have to be smart and take care of myself. Living with RA has changed how I do a lot of things. I have to think about consequences more. If I do this, then, what am I going to have to pay for it? For example, if I spend a couple of hours shopping or at lunch with a friend I know I will be in pain, probably won't sleep and will likely be in bed at least part of the next day. I have to decide if the payment is worth the benefit. Sometimes it is; sometimes it isn't. But, there is the God factor that I cannot ignore. In my logical thinking, going to China to build a church would naturally equate to severe pain, extreme exhaustion and several days in bed. However, God intervenes for me and gives me divine strength and renewal that helps me do the task without the consequences or with extremely limited consequences.

It is eye-opening and rather scary to think about how we respond to life and the decisions we make when our perspective is skewed by exhaustion – mental, emotional, spiritual and/or physical. One of the difficult things is recognizing when our perspective is being affected. I've spent a lot of time coaching others about perspective and thinking about it, so I can usually recognize it. However, I know a lot of people who make really bad decisions over and over again because their perspective is messed up.

In order to diagnose potential skewed perspective, think about the following questions. Each of these individually can lead to distortion in our perception of events, however, when two or more are present, the distortion increases.

Are you physically exhausted? (This can be due to life circumstances, work schedule, busyness, illness, etc.)	❒ Yes ❒ No
Are you feeling pressure from either yourself or others to do something?	❒ Yes ❒ No
Are you unusually emotional? (Are little things causing you to respond emotionally?)	❒ Yes ❒ No
Are you feeling conflicted between what you are actually doing and your life priorities or values?	❒ Yes ❒ No
Are you ill? (This can be a short-term illness, chronic condition or life-threatening disease, or the perception of having a severe physical problem.)	❒ Yes ❒ No
Is your stress level higher than normal or has it been high for a lengthy amount of time?	❒ Yes ❒ No
Have you recently experienced a tragic event or significant loss?	❒ Yes ❒ No
Are you having financial difficulties?	❒ Yes ❒ No
Are you having problems at work? (Conflict with boss or co-workers, loss of customer, unachievable expectations, disciplinary issues, etc.)	❒ Yes ❒ No

If one or more of the above conditions exist, you should pause before making any important decisions. It is extremely beneficial to use a decision making process any time you are making decisions, especially so when you are making decisions in a difficult time. A simple process is:

1. Ask questions to gain a better understanding of the problem to be solved or decision to be made. What exactly needs to be decided? Why does a decision need to be made? What will happen if I don't make a decision? What caused the current situation? What is the root cause of the problem or situation needing to be addressed?
2. Propose solutions or options. What choices do you have? Write them down. Don't analyze or discount any solutions at this point. Just make a list. Sometimes the craziest ideas end up being the best solution or a trigger to help you find the best solution. This is also a great time to have an accountability partner work with you to identify your options. Two heads really are better than one.
3. Evaluate each option. What are the potential outcomes of each option? Think about both short term and long term consequences and benefits of each option. How does the option fit with your values and priorities?
4. Decide the best option based on the potential outcomes. Pray and ask God to give you direction. Sometimes the decision God wants you to make is not the one that looks the best on paper.
5. Implement the plan. After you decide *what* to do, you have to actually do it. Knowing what to do and actually doing it are two different things. Again, this is a great time to involve an accountability partner to help you take the step.

~ Just Be ~

What does this 'rest' mean? For me, it means I have to think about what I do. Take care of myself but trust God to help me when He asks me to do something that would normally wipe me out.

God gives us strength, hope and peace in the waiting. Trust Him even when life is hard and the battles are fierce. Find joy in Him when life brings anything but joy. Count on Him to bring peace in the middle of distress. He is your life-line. Hold onto Him.

Sometimes our thoughts can be suffocating – what if – how can we – will it work – will we survive – is God going to do something before we crash and burn? They can suffocate life right out of our body leaving us with fear, doubt, confusion, sleeplessness. Nothing good. So what can we do? The only thing I know is taking control of those thoughts and getting them out of my head. Replace those thoughts with thoughts about God. Even thoughts about good things can be consuming. When our mind is jumping from one thought to the next, there is no rest, no peace. Let your mind be still. Still functioning but in a state of stillness. A place where your mind is fixed on God even in the midst of daily life. Open for God to speak rather than so busy with random thoughts drowning Him out. I wish there was a magic switch to turn our brain from go-go-go to stillness. There is nothing more peaceful than being still in mind and body when the stillness is centered on Jesus. Just 'be'.

Exodus 14:14 The Lord will fight for you; you need only to be still.

Quite often, I think I need to fill my days more so I can feel productive and worthwhile, like I'm contributing. Wow! What a huge distraction! I don't need to add more stuff. I need to choose the right stuff and let my body and mind be still instead.

Have you ever coughed so much and so hard you couldn't breathe? Every attempt at taking a breath results in more coughing. I've experienced that a few times. Recently, I had a cold I brought home from Ecuador. One night as I was trying to go to sleep, I started coughing and couldn't stop. Then, I couldn't breathe at all and I started to feel panicky. I told myself, "slow down, take easy breaths, relax, be still." Before long, the attack stopped. I need to do the same process with life stuff too.

> *Exodus 33:13 If you are pleased with me, teach me your ways so I may know you and continue to find favor with you. Remember that this nation is your people." 14 The Lord replied, "My Presence will go with you, and I will give you rest." (NLT — Please, if this is really so, show me your intentions so I will understand you more fully and do exactly what you want me to do. Besides, don't forget that this nation is your very own people." 14 And the LORD replied, "I will personally go with you, Moses. I will give you rest – everything will be fine for you.")*

Sometimes my mind gets wrapped up in questions. A lot of the questions don't really matter. The ones that do are, "Am I doing what I'm supposed to be doing – my God-ordained calling?" and "Do I trust God with everything?" All the other questions are insignificant. I frequently have no idea how we will get through the battles we are facing. But, I do know God never fails and He is the one in control. Does anything else really matter?

I read or reflect on Psalm 118 almost every day. I use these words to get my mind focused on God instead of the chaos of life. This is my passageway from a busy mind to a mind still with a single focus. As I read, I speak it out loud as a prayer.

Psalm 118: 1 Give thanks to the LORD, for he is good! His faithful love endures forever. 2 Let the congregation of Israel repeat: "His faithful love endures forever." 3 Let Aaron's descendants, the priests, repeat: "His faithful love endures forever." 4 Let all who fear the LORD repeat: "His faithful love endures forever." 5 In my distress I prayed to the LORD, and the LORD answered me and rescued me. 6 The LORD is for me, so I will not be afraid. What can mere mortals do to me? 7 Yes, the LORD is for me; he will help me. I will look in triumph at those who hate me. 8 It is better to trust the LORD than to put confidence in people. 9 It is better to trust the LORD than to put confidence in princes. 10 Though hostile nations surrounded me, I destroyed them all in the name of the LORD. 11 Yes, they surrounded and attacked me, but I destroyed them all in the name of the LORD. 12 They swarmed around me like bees; they blazed against me like a roaring flame. But I destroyed them all in the name of the LORD. 13 You did your best to kill me, O my enemy, but the LORD helped me. 14 The LORD is my strength and my song; he has become my victory. 15 Songs of joy and victory are sung in the camp of the godly. The strong right arm of the LORD has done glorious things! 16 The strong right arm of the LORD is raised in triumph. The strong right arm of the LORD has done glorious things! 17 I will not die, but I will live to tell what the LORD has done. 18 The LORD has punished me severely, but he has not handed me over to death.

19 Open for me the gates where the righteous enter, and I will go in and thank the LORD. 20 Those gates lead to the presence of the LORD, and the godly enter there. 21 I thank you for answering my prayer and saving me! 22 The stone rejected by the builders has now become the cornerstone. 23 This is the LORD's doing, and it is marvelous to see. 24 This is the day the LORD has made. We will rejoice and be glad in it. 25 Please, LORD, please save us. Please, LORD, please give us success. 26 Bless the one who comes in the name of the LORD. We bless you from the house of the LORD. 27 The LORD is God, shining upon us. Bring forward the sacrifice and put it on the altar. 28 You are my God, and I will praise you! You are my God, and I will exalt you! 29 Give thanks to the LORD, for he is good! His faithful love endures forever.

In this Psalm, David is confident in the goodness and power of God. I can sense his confidence and exuberance as I read the verses. He has seen the Lord do great things and give him victory in battle. David had a big view of God – He recognized God's awesome power and authority. Take comfort in the fact God is really big and is in absolute control at all times.

Whether you are in the middle of a difficult time in life or you are in the best time of your life, it is okay to rest. Take time to care for yourself. Take the hot bubble bath you wish you had time for. Read the book you've been waiting to read. Take a nap. Whatever is relaxing for you, make time to do it. I have a friend who has repeatedly told me – if you don't take care of yourself, you are no good to anyone else. Nourish your body with food and nourish your spirit with lingering time with the Lord.

Chapter 9 – So, Have You Ever Felt Like Habakkuk?

Habakkuk 3:17-19 Though the fig tree does not blossom and there is no fruit on the vines, [though] the product of the olive fails and the fields yield no food, though the flock is cut off from the fold and there are no cattle in the stalls, Yet I will rejoice in the Lord; I will exult in the [victorious] God of my salvation! The Lord God is my Strength, my personal bravery, and my invincible army; He makes my feet like hinds' feet and will make me to walk [not to stand still in terror, but to walk] and make [spiritual] progress upon my high places [of trouble, suffering, or responsibility]! (Amplified Bible)

Can you relate to Habakkuk? I can. Or, what about Job, who lost his animals, his servants and his children. He lost so much. Hurting, hit hard, helpless, reeling from the blow. Have you been to a place where nothing seems to be going right? When you're there, how do you respond?

Habakkuk is surrounded by violence, destruction, grief and injustice. He complains to God about what he sees around him. God responds to Habakkuk by explaining His plan for dealing with the trouble Habakkuk sees. In Habakkuk 1:6, the Lord says, "I am rousing up the Chaldeans, that bitter and impetuous nation who march through the breadth of the earth to take possession of dwelling places that do not belong to them." (Amplified Bible) God's plan was to use the Chaldeans to judge the Israelites. Habakkuk's response is a hearty, "Lord, you've got to be kidding me! What are you thinking?" Have you ever felt the same way? After conversing with the Lord, Habakkuk essentially says he will listen to what the Lord says and will accept it and he will be obedient. Then, comes Habakkuk's prayer in chapter three. He describes the fear and distress he has experienced but Habakkuk doesn't stop there. He talks about the victory the Lord brings. "Yet I will rejoice in the Lord; I will exult in the [victorious] God of my salvation! The Lord God is my Strength, my personal bravery and my invincible army."

It seems like it is always the silliest things that put most of us over the edge. One year – the whole summer – our brand new, top-of-the-line washing machine was broken. After four technician visits and four different diagnosis of the problem, we finally knew what was wrong. Unfortunately, the part was back-ordered – for four months! At the same time, we were waiting to hear from the IRS to get our tax-exempt status approved for our missions organization. Not to mention the normal RA stuff. On top of that, Taylor was having a terrible time at school with one of his teachers and he was becoming depressed. The teacher was far from understanding, was not flexible and told Taylor she didn't like him. Ok – that made me mad! He struggled in her classes, even though they were his favorite and best subjects – math and science. We had several weeks where he wouldn't even turn in work because he was afraid to ask her questions. And then, the last little shove over the edge – a flat tire. Most of the time, piling on of things cause us to crumble more than a single horrific event.

Many days I have to sit back and just laugh at what has transpired. At one of my doctor's appointments, I explained to my rheumatologist how bad of a month it had been. She continued her normal exam and we discussed trying a different treatment. Then, I told her about another pain I was experiencing around my chest and back and a rash that appeared the previous day. She looked and just shook her head. She told me I had shingles, which meant I couldn't be on any of my RA medications until it was gone. I just burst out laughing. I couldn't stop. Next thing I know, she's laughing too. My choice was either laugh or cry. I am my doctor's problem child, so she understood and just laughed with me.

I felt like I was hanging over a cliff with just the tips of my toes hanging on. I look back at all the times I asked God why the answer is taking so long and feeling like we were not going to make it. Two years later I was saying the same thing. I didn't see how we could make it but we did. But, we were just at the beginning of learning to truly live by faith. At the point when I first felt like we were in the storm, I never realized we weren't even close to the fringe of the storm, much less the epi-center. Let me give you some advice. When you are in the heat of a battle, don't ever say it can't get worse. It can and likely will. But, don't give up because God is really really big!

We tend to limit God in our minds. Our view of God defines us. If we have a small view of God, we don't expect much. We live bigger as we have a bigger view of God. When we see Him as our strength, we can live in His strength and not our own. When we understand how big He is – bigger than we can truly comprehend – the little things in life pale in comparison to Him. The things we think are big problems suddenly seem small. So, what is your view of God? How does your view of God impact the way you live? Where are you limiting God in your life?

Maybe the answer you need seems to be taking a long time to arrive. You've trusted. You've waited. You've put your hope in God. But, it seems like all you get back is more trouble, more pain, more heartache and more desperation. God does not want you to give up. I have asked God if He really has a plan for us or if we have we been fooled. Sometimes all I see is the hurt, pain, heartache, need, ruin. Be careful to not dwell in these thoughts too long. These thoughts will lead to an inwardly focused mind. A mind living like the battle is lost. Job does this same thing for a while. In fact, in Job 3, he curses the day he was born and complained about his misery. After repeated discouraging conversations with his so-called friends, Job must have felt totally deflated. Have you been there? I know I have had conversations with friends who I was certain would encourage me but I left feeling worse than I did before the conversation.

> *Job 26:14 And these are but the outer fringe of his works; how faint the whisper we hear of him! Who then can understand the thunder of his power?"*

Jesus has already paid the price to crush the attacks of our enemy. The LORD is the Almighty God and there is nothing that can stand against us when He is on our side.

Dear master potter of this clay,
Make me into what is pleasing to you.
Break me and start over where needed.
Help me to display the splendor of your greatness.
I feel myself trying to take control. Should I?
I feel myself questioning. Am I wrong?
I feel myself self-destructing. How can I stop it?
I need answers. Will you give them?
Trials give us strength and character.
There's so much to do and so little time to do it in.
I feel paralyzed and useless.

I am too driven and too passionate to be in this
paralyzed state.
You are the dream giver and the dream fulfiller.
I am counting on you to get me through this.

In the middle of huge wars and daily life, we can feel so overwhelmed. We can even wonder if God cares. If this is where you are, stop. Go back to the Elijah process – rest, eat, spend time with God and gain some perspective. Now, look at your view of God.

Habakkuk didn't focus on the empty trees, crops, sheep pens and cattle stalls. He identified the problem. He stated the facts, <u>yet</u>, he rejoiced in the Lord. Why? Because God is his savior, He is sovereign, the Lord is his strength and the Lord enables him to go upon the high places. Habakkuk knows things aren't right or good but he chooses to focus on God.

When we are in situations like Habakkuk or Job, there will be decisions to make. We would really like for God to just tell us what to do. Every time I pray, the answer I get from God is trust me. In the Bible, you see Joshua and David and so many others ask God what to do...this or that...and God tells them do this. When you ask and He says "trust me," which choice do you make? Well, Taylor says, keep waiting until God says which choice to make. Sounds like good advice to me.

Sometimes we need to just stop what we're doing and wait in the valley for a bit. Learn from it. Maybe the lesson isn't something about us. (I know it's hard to believe everything isn't about us.) Maybe the lesson is about God. This valley may be an opportunity to learn a new aspect of God we've never paid attention to before or have never personally experienced before. Maybe as we are in the valley, we have opportunities to come alongside someone else who is in their own valley and to partner with them and strengthen them. I firmly believe it is critical for each of us to find some way to use challenges, difficulties and heartaches in our own life to help someone else. The result may be we are just more compassionate for others. We may be able to pray more effectively for someone else experiencing a similar trial. Let your experiences grow you and enable you to build up others.

Chapter 10 – Just Trust Me

Psalm 9:10 Those who know your name will trust in you, for you, Lord, have never forsaken those who seek you.

Go ahead and tell me; you can trust me. Have you heard those words before? Usually when I hear those words, blaring sirens go off in my head warning me to be cautious. Some people say 'trust me' because they are nosy and want to know things they shouldn't. Others say 'trust me' with good intentions but don't follow through with what they promise. Then, there are others who say 'trust me' and prove themselves to be trustworthy. But there is no person who is as trustworthy as God.

At times it feels like we never make any progress. We get tired of fighting. I've had days where I felt maxed out on the amount I can carry, past what I can bear. It seemed like each day was just like the day before which was like the day before and the day two years ago. Nothing has changed except we have less money; my health is worse; we're older; we have more people who we want to help but can't and we are one step closer to being buried alive. Will I feel differently tomorrow? Probably. *I'll* just deal with it. *I'll* 'man up'. Wait. Who is our trust in when we respond this way? Me or God? I know God is bigger and more powerful and has more authority than anything else in existence. He is the one in whom our trust must be.

Trust means "reliance on the integrity, strength, ability, surety, etc., of a person; confident expectation of something; hope."[xi] When we are trusting God, we are relying on someone who is perfect, who never fails, who is always faithful, who never lets us down and who is always looking out for our best interest. Trusting God means believing He will do what He has promised and not worrying about it or trying to figure things out on our own. It's easy to say we trust God but how many times do we say those words and then, proceed to try to handle things ourselves or worry about what is going to happen. Absolute trust, expectant trust, confident trust is a lesson Jimmy and I have learned the past year. We had to let go of all control. We had to let go of our uncertainties. We had to let go of our own plans. Then, we had to just rest in unwavering trust in God Almighty.

For the past three years God has repeatedly answered our prayers by just saying trust me. After a while, I would respond back – yeah I know that – I do trust you. Now, what are we supposed to do? "Trust me." You see, trusting God is the activity we do. Trusting is active. When we 'trust' God and then try to do things on our own or use our own strength, we are not really trusting Him. I have to go back and read through my list of who God is and realize – I don't have to worry or try to fix things myself – God is the one in control and He can do anything.

Those who are totally committed to God to the point of going against the norm, those who are taking a risk for God, will face tragic, testing, stormy situations. What will the response be? Shadrach, Meshach and Abednego were committed to God regardless of the circumstance. They said they would still serve God even if He doesn't rescue them. Live or die, they were committed. Then God showed up and provided the answer even after the King had them thrown into the fiery furnace. At what point does the answer come? Is it when personally we can't survive another day or when we have completely failed? When does the answer come? The answer always comes in the exact moment it is supposed to come.

When we were selling our house, I was so sure it would sell the first week. So, we started packing and getting ourselves ready to move. Well, eight months later we were still in the house. We finally got a contract on the house with a closing date set two weeks later. Woohoo! We thought we were certainly making progress and things were finally moving forward. Well, it was a nice idea but not the reality. The closing was scheduled and postponed and scheduled and postponed for more than two months we waited. We were counting on the money from the sale of the house for our survival. It's hard to trust when things aren't going according to our plan. Sometimes it may seem like God is answering everyone's prayers but yours. You keep waiting and waiting. All God says is to trust Him. When it seems nothing is going right, remember who is on your side. We finally closed on the house two months after our original closing date. Even though the entire lengthy process was not what we planned or what we thought it would be, we could see God working. These ten months were excruciatingly stressful, especially as we neared the end. But, during this time we experienced miracles and divine appointments that stretched our understanding of God. I would not want to relive those months but I would not trade the growth I experienced.

Each day is a gift – even the bad days. During the bad days, I sometimes struggle to see what is good about it. But, I see God working in those days. There were so many days I could barely get out of bed but with God's help, I did. I went to work. He gave me the words to say to make a difference in my clients' businesses, in the people. He gave me strength to be on my feet all day. He helped me have the strength to go to Jamaica, Mexico, Romania, Fiji, China, Ecuador, Honduras, Colombia and more. It wasn't me. I didn't have an ounce of strength. But, He did. In my weakness, He was and is strong. Even in the middle of the fiercest storm, God worked in my life. I wouldn't trade one of those days because they have made me who I am. They have helped me to know God in ways I couldn't have otherwise. As I trust Him and He proves faithful, my hope and trust in Him grows. I have experienced more pain, fear, hope, faith, despair, aloneness, connectedness, exhaustion, helplessness, anger, joy, confusion and peace the past two years than any time before. It has been a time of dichotomies.

Throughout 2007, we frequently only had pennies in our bank account. No food in the refrigerator, no money for our mortgage payment, for gas, for bills but God. But God – provided. On one of the no money days in the Fall of 2007, Jimmy's computer died. I was physically in such constantly intense pain I felt like I was out of hope but God provided again. God provided a new computer for Jimmy and gave me a renewed tolerance for my pain. The sources of provision from God were so varied and often from unexpected sources. Even now as I think back to the past two years, I am amazed at the variety of sources God has used to sustain us. I never expected to be eating government food, worrying about past due bills and getting loans from friends. We have felt humiliated and blessed at the same time.

Jimmy, Taylor and I drove to Dallas in the summer of 2008 for a meeting about fundraising for Clear Vision Ministries. This was a quick down to Dallas and back to Wichita. We stopped to eat at the Redneck Café – yes, that is the name of the place. It was actually pretty good southern food. So, with our bellies full and the meeting behind us, we headed home on what should have been about a six-hour drive. We crossed over the Texas/Oklahoma border and about forty miles later our car died. It just stopped running. We were at an exit when the death happened, so Jimmy put the car in neutral and coasted down the exit. With the car dead, he had to put significant force into making the turn after the stop sign that he ran. As he turned, we saw a gas station right in front of us. We finally roll into the parking lot of the gas station and the diagnosis process began. You know how this works – you open the hood and look in as if you know what you're looking for. Then, you shake your head, shrug your shoulders, touch something, then, something else, all the while looking like you know what you're doing. Well, after Jimmy did this for a few minutes, one of the station employees came out and asked if he could help. Accepting the offer, Jimmy explained what happened and the diagnosis process resumed. Our helper mimicked many of the same movements Jimmy had already completed. After about an hour, they determined there was a problem with the engine. Jimmy called a wrecker and I called my mom to pray for us. I explained what happened and where we were. My mom, after conferring with my dad, told me dad had a cousin in a town nearby. Mom gave me the telephone number for my dad's cousin and assured me she would be able to help us get to town and find a place to stay for the night. We sat at a table inside the gas station for almost three hours waiting for the wrecker to show up. Finally the wrecker gets there and hooks up the car. There is only room for Jimmy to ride in the wrecker cab. Now Jimmy was gone and Taylor and I were stranded at the gas station. We're in the middle of nowhere and I have no idea exactly where Jimmy is going. My cell phone battery was dead, so I ask our new friend at the station if I can plug in behind the counter. I plug in and dial the number of my dad's cousin who I had never met. I honestly did not expect to get any help from this related stranger. She didn't know me. But, she came. We were completely astounded by her kindness. Instead of dropping us off at a hotel, she brought us to her house. We enjoyed a lot of conversation, good food and true southern hospitality. We did in fact lose the engine in the car but we gained some new family members! Two days later, we left the car to be repaired and rented a car to drive home. With no idea how we would pay for the repairs, all we could do was trust God. On the day we left home to go pick up the car, God provided the exact dollar amount we needed to pay for our new engine. We trusted and God did not abandon us.

After our car ordeal, a couple weeks later I was at home and heard this humming sound. After a few seconds the humming sounded more like a piece of machinery groaning, then, back to a low hum. So, I walk through the house to find what is making the dreadful noise. It's the sump pump. At this point in the morning, we had about 3 inches of rain. The sump pump hole was full and not emptying. When Jimmy got home, he messed around with it for a while and got it working again. He basically got lucky because he had no clue what he was doing! A couple hours later, I was in my closet praying and heard this thumping noise. I thought Jimmy was trying to get my attention, so I opened the door to see water dripping from our light fixture! At this point it had rained about 5 inches and the wind was blowing the rain sideways. It had apparently blown rain through the vents on the top of the house. After Jimmy removed the light fixture, the rain dripped a while and finally stopped. I decided to look through the other rooms and found a spot in the guest room upstairs that was filling up with water. Jimmy poked a hole in the ceiling with a straight pin to allow the rain to drip out. It did and then, we dried the ceiling with a hairdryer. On the same day, I braved the 8" rain to buy pinto beans so we could eat that week. I get home and I'm rinsing the beans and as I drain the water, I drop the bowl and spill the beans down the garbage disposal. Yep, this was definitely a day to remember. At this point, I just started laughing. I couldn't help but wonder if we would survive the day. Have you ever had a day where everything imaginable and many things unimaginable go wrong? We may be tempted to quit. We may even have people like Job's wife tell us to "curse God and die." Our relationship with God leads us to trust Him even on the bad days. While we do not see the future and how things will work out, God does. He knows exactly what will happen and how the pieces fit together.

There is a paradox within me. There's the 'I believe, I trust, I know God will provide and answer' and the 'I can't handle this anymore, how will we make it another day, I can't even breathe.' It is from this place we must choose. Will we hang on to what we believe and know to be truth or how we feel?

God is constant. Friends come and go. Situations are temporary. God is always there. He is constant. He doesn't change. He doesn't go away. When everything else fails, we can still count on God. He is constant even when your emotions and state of mind are out of control. God doesn't change based on how we feel. Frankly, our emotions have nothing to do with establishing God's actual character or ability. If we rely on our emotions as a barometer of God's love, power and ability, then, we are destined for a rough ride full of disappointment.

Not only is God constant regardless of our emotions and state of mind, He is also constant when we fail or are unfaithful to Him. What we do does not change who He is.

Many times I've thought 'what's the point!' We have no hope, no future, no chance of success unless God steps in. It's the 'unless' part that is always the key. Then, we are torn between what we see and what we believe to be true. I may feel defeated but I know God has already won the battle. God fights for us because we cannot do it on our own.

It's in the darkest times we have an opportunity to shine the brightest. It is our response to those times that shows who we really are and what is important to us. A friend so appropriately said, "the light doesn't shine too bright until it's really dark." He was talking about an actual light but how true it is about our lives shining in a really dark world.

> *Hebrews 10:23 - Let us hold fast the confession of our hope without wavering, for He who promised is faithful.*

It is not beyond God's capability to pour out blessings in astonishing ways. Whatever comes our way is nothing compared to God's power and greatness. Our job is to live in his greatness and power and to share it with others. When we live in God's power and greatness, we live life differently.

In the face of adversity, pray and keep going. Trust God without any doubt, just as Nehemiah did when rebuilding the wall. While building the wall, enemies of Jerusalem plotted attacks on Nehemiah and his fellow builders. I am inspired as I read in Nehemiah chapter 4 verse 17 where the workers are working with one hand and holding a weapon in the other. The workers, following Nehemiah's leadership, were not intimidated or slowed down by threats of attack.

After Nehemiah fasted and prayed (Nehemiah 1), he praised God who keeps His promises to those who love and obey Him. Then, he asked God to hear his prayer, confessed his sins, reminded God of His promise and asked for success by granting him favor in the presence of the king. God fulfilled all Nehemiah asked and more. He exceeded Nehemiah's request.

When we were building one of the churches in China, a new and dear friend started calling me "Mrs. Nehemiah." How cool is that! As I stood on rickety scaffolding made of two really old and frail looking school desks and two slabs of some kind of pressed wood-like material, I certainly had no trust whatsoever in the capability of the scaffolding to keep my 5'2" 120 pound body from falling to the ground! But, I held in my left hand a brick and in my right hand a trowel full of mortar. My hands were busy laying brick while my feet were trying to not fall off or through the scaffolding. My thoughts were on the people who would walk through the doors and the worship that would be lifted up to the Almighty within the walls we were building. You see, whatever we do in life, the eternal things are what really matter. When we place our complete trust in I AM, when we follow His direction, when our focus is on the things in life that matter, we become a conduit for I AM.

As we live our life, there are a lot of things we've learned to trust so much we don't even think about it. When we flip a light switch, we expect the light to come on. We don't stand there and wonder if it will come on or not. We expect if we eat food we will not be hungry. If we turn a faucet, water will come out. We trust so easily in those things. You don't realize it until they don't work. Our first week in the Galapagos, we stayed at a really cool hotel operated by a local family. Water on the islands is pumped by electricity; it's not typical running water like we would expect in the US. We were getting instructions on how to heat up the water for our showers. Here's the instructions we received: "Turn the water on all the way. Then, when the light flickers, turn the water down until the light flickers again. That is when it will be hot." I thought the directions sounded easy enough. The showerhead has a little pump-like unit attached to it and it is plugged into an electrical outlet. So, I turn the water on and look around the showerhead for the light that is supposed to flicker. I can't find the light. Then, all the sudden, all the lights in the hotel room flicker. It hits me that there isn't a light on the showerhead, the light I'm looking for is the room light. I felt like a complete idiot but who knew the room light was the indication the water was hot! When we got home, I didn't look around at lights to determine the temperature of the water. I automatically trusted what I knew to be true — turn the knob for hot water and I would get hot water.

The next week we are in an apartment on a different island in the Galapagos. Again, the water is pumped by electricity. We walked into the apartment and there was no electricity. We turned on water and nothing came out of the faucet. For several hours, there was no water or electricity. Finally, it came back on that night. Then randomly every day, there would be moments or hours where there was no electricity or water. So, each time I flipped a light switch or turned a faucet I wondered if it was going to work.

God is more trustworthy than electricity. He works in every country consistently without blackouts. He doesn't just work in developed countries or for people of specific status. He is always working. He is. He does not cease His trustworthiness at any time. We can always without exception trust Him.

How do you live life and get through the storms – How do you trust God?

1) Focus on who God is, not circumstances – I read my list of who God is every day. Experience God. You ALWAYS HAVE A CHOICE of where you place your focus.
2) Get rid of things that take your focus off of God, what distracts you – maybe you need a change of scenery. When you feel the storm raging – stop and assess your focus. Maybe you focus on 'good things' but not God.
3) Don't give up – fight the urge to quit or worry or take control yourself. This means you have to make a decision to not give up – make a decision to trust God.
4) Cognitively reprogram your thoughts to live life like God has already provided the answer. This means you intentionally change your thoughts and perception,

which influence our behaviors, attitudes and actions. What we think directly influences our attitudes, behaviors and how we feel about life.

5) Create a support system – This is what friends are for. If you don't have a friend who is in the same space, then, confide in a trustworthy friend who will pray for you and listen to you. Let people help you.
6) Look for purpose in the storm – can you use what you are learning to help someone else? What can you learn about God during the storm?

All of these things require being INTENTIONAL in how you live and how you process life and how you view God. Trust Him.

Chapter 11 – Jesus, Please Make Me More Like You

Ephesians 1: 18 I pray that your hearts will be flooded with light so that you can understand the confident hope he has given to those he called—his holy people who are his rich and glorious inheritance. 19 I also pray that you will understand the incredible greatness of God's power for us who believe him. This is the same mighty power

More of you, Lord
More of you
No matter what the cost
I want to reach the lost
So they can know more of you
Lord, more of you
Mold me and make me a vessel you can use
Empty me of me
Then fill me with more of you
More of you, Lord
More of you
You're my strength and shield
Thank you for being so real
I want to know more of you
Lord, more of you
You are the lifter of my head

You bring joy to my soul
You're the strength of my life
My friend through this fight
Great is your love, Lord
As I walk through this valley
The spring is just in sight
More of you, Lord
More of you
You are faithful and true
You make this passion renewed
To know more of you, Lord
More of you
In complete awe of you ~

When you are close enough to God to hear His heart beating, you cannot help but be compelled to be more like Him. The more I reflect and internalize who He is, the more I realize I need to be more like Him. I need to be more of a servant. I need to be more compassionate, have more grace, live in peace, have hope, be deeper, love freely, die to myself, use wisdom, be supportive, not worry about what others think and so much more.

It's kind of like holding a strong magnet in one hand and a piece of metal in the other. The closer you move the metal to the magnet, the more the metal is drawn to the magnet. Then, you get close enough and the metal is sucked onto the magnet. With enough exposure, the metal can become magnetized. It can take on the properties of the magnet.

In our effort to be more like Jesus, we first have to know what He is like. As we know His character, we can then begin to allow Him to develop His character in our own lives. Have you ever noticed how much you act like the people you are around the most? If you have kids, you have probably had times when your son or daughter has acted just like you or just like your spouse.

I enjoy painting walls. I'm too messy to be confined to artistic painting on a canvas. Walls are big and I can be creative but I am always messy. I end up with paint on my clothes, hands, face and my tarp has drops all over it but the wall looks good in the end. This is a trait I have somehow passed on to Taylor. When we were in Romania, we painted benches at a village church and a wall at the missionary's house. Taylor and I both had red paint in numerous places. He bumped into the paint, kneeled in a drop of paint and had paint all over his hands. Like mother, like son. He's also like Jimmy in a lot of ways. He spends time with us, watches us, learns from us and takes on our characteristics.

Likeness to Christ comes through time with Him. You cannot expect to become like Him or anyone else without a significant investment of time and energy. There is not a quick three-step, two-minute plan to change your life. It is a lifelong journey with sacrificial investment of time and your life. You may think this sounds a little hard. It needs to sound hard because it is hard. It requires work. It requires commitment. It requires time. It requires rearranging priorities.

I know people who will do anything for God as long as they do not have to change how they live their lives. As Jesus called the disciples to follow Him, they left their life as they knew it. They had to sacrifice everything to follow the Messiah. They walked all over the place; they had no home; they didn't have a steady income; they got dirty. They were with Jesus day and night. How many days do we have where we try to squeeze our God-time into a 10-minute window as we are rushing to do the next thing on our list? A rushed, when I have time for it kind of relationship will not lead you to a place where you are close enough to God to hear His heart beating, nor will it transform you to be more like Him.

Being more like Jesus is really about a transformation of our core being. This type of transformation affects our thoughts, desires, actions, words, relationships, decisions, everything. It is about who we are and what we do. Do you have compassion? Does it drive you to action? Do you show grace and mercy regardless of the offense? Are you a servant or do you expect others to serve you? These are tough questions. Think about them honestly.

As we seek to be more like Jesus, we must proactively chase Him. We can't pause because of barriers. We must be persistent. Ask. Listen. Obey. Ask for complete understanding of His will.

Here are a few of the things I've learned about Jesus. As you read through the list, think about how you have seen Him. He is:

- I AM
- Everlasting God – He doesn't go away.
- Our hope for the present and our future.
- The Creator of all things big and small.
- Working God – He is continually working in our lives, in the world, to fulfill His will.
- Faithful and dependable – You can always count on God.
- Infallible – He does not make mistakes.
- Good – He is the personification of good.
- Purposeful – Everything He does has a purpose.
- Healer – He paid the price for our healing.
- Restorer – He puts back together the things that are broken within us.
- Holy – There is not one speck of unholiness in Him.
- Pure – He is authentically genuine.
- Creative – He is the master at creativity. Look around you.
- Omniscient – He knows all things.
- Wisdom – He has complete understanding and perception of all things.
- Captain of the Lord of Hosts – He's in charge of heaven's armies.

- The calmer of storms.
- Always present – He never walks away from us.
- Incomparable – There is no one like Him.
- Our Teacher – He enables us to learn everything we need to know.
- Unwearied – He never gets tired or worn down.
- Our tower and shield
- Precious – He is more precious than the finest gems.
- Gentle – While He is powerful, He is tender.
- A true servant
- Merciful
- Compassionate – He deeply cares for us and is profoundly concerned about us.
- Gracious – He is kind and benevolent.
- Forgiver – He forgives to the uttermost.
- Friend – He is our very best friend and companion.
- Our freedom – He sets us free from whatever might bind us.
- Powerful – He is the ultimate power source in the universe.
- In Control – He has all things under control and in control.
- Supreme authority – There is no one higher than Him.
- Sovereign – He rules and reigns supreme without the need of committees to guide Him.
- Love – His love is complete and abundant.
- Constant – He doesn't waver. He is continuous, relentless, loyal.
- Prayer Answering God – He hears and answers our prayers.
- Mediator – He arbitrates on our behalf.
- The truth – He defines truth.

- Unforgetting – He has no memory loss. All things at all times for all people are always present in His mind.
- Our foundation – He is the rock that holds our feet firm.
- Infinite – He lives on forever and has no limits on His capabilities.
- Our sacrifice – He willingly laid down His life for us.
- Majestic – He is the most magnificent royalty.
- Awesome – He is breathtakingly awe-inspiring.
- Lord of Heaven & Earth – He rules.
- Lord of All – He reigns.
- Joy of my heart.
- My inspiration.
- Victorious in all things.

I'm so glad God is who He is in spite of who I am. Sometimes I feel so under-talented and ill suited for the things we do. But, it is not our skills and abilities that are necessary to complete the task. It is God in us. He equips us to do what He calls us to do. When we rely on Him and completely trust Him, He does things through us we never thought possible. We are still responsible for learning and preparing but our trust needs to be in God, not our education, talents or preparations.

One of the most difficult things about traveling to third world and developing countries is coming back to the USA. I get fed up with selfishness. We all fall into the trap periodically and some never leave. Do I want stuff? Sure. But, I want Jesus more. Is wanting stuff bad? No, as long as it is in the right priority level. Really, we are so blessed in the USA. Even in tough times we are surrounded by excess. Excess frequently fills our lives so much we squeeze God out. As we seek to be more like Jesus, our attention and focus has to move away from self and stuff.

In my journey to be more like Jesus, I asked Him to show me the non-Christ-like things in my life. Be prepared to see some ugly things. For me, I saw a need for more grace with those I love. I need more gentleness and less using a big stick. I need to be a servant to everyone. I find it easy to serve our missionaries, the people we encounter on our missions projects, our friends. But, sometimes I get tired and don't feel like being a servant for my family. After seeing the things I need to change, I started paying attention more to my daily behavior, responses to things and the words I say. I catch myself being a little light on grace and ask the Lord to help me show grace. Whatever your growing points are, Jesus is with you and is willing and able to help you become more like Him. We always have room to grow and change to become more like Jesus. Rather than identifying *if* we need to change or grow, the real question we need to ask is *what do we need to change or in what area do we need to grow*.

Change and growth are both processes. I understand sometimes change and growth can be instantaneous but the majority of times it is an ongoing process. Process means time, effort, decision and determination must be present. The first step in change is becoming aware of the need for change. You can't change something you don't know needs to be changed. After awareness, the next step is identifying specifically what changes are necessary – either what you need to stop doing, start doing or do differently. Then, begin replacing the old behavior with new behavior. Change is easier when you replace one behavior with another instead of just trying to eliminate the original behavior.

I love change. In fact, I become restless when change is absent. There are not very many people in the world who embrace change, especially when they are the subject of the change. If you want to be more like Jesus, change is going to be part of your life. You may not like the process but it is necessary. As we are more like Jesus in the core of our being, I believe we hear His heart beating clearer and stronger. What changes do you need to make in your life? Where is God trying to grow you?

Chapter 12 – Fulfilling God's Plan

2 Timothy 2:2 You have heard me teach many things that have been confirmed by many reliable witnesses. Teach these great truths to trustworthy people who are able to pass them on to others.

~ My Journey ~

I absolutely love the ocean, beaches and the sound of waves. The sound of the waves washing up on the beach is soothing. The heat from the sun feels so good to me. It actually helps my joint pain to lessen for a while. The beach is the ultimate relaxation spot for me. However, I cannot swim. I would like to but the water terrifies me. In March 2008, we were in Tela, Honduras. To get to the beach area we were visiting for a site seeing excursion, we had to ride in this tiny boat across choppy waters. There were several times when I was certain the boat was going to tip over and of course, I would die in the "middle of the ocean." The boat ride took about 40 minutes but it seemed like an eternity. Every time I thought I was getting used to the bouncing, swaying ride, we would be smacked. Waves would hit us and it would feel like we were toppling over – all I could see was the wave. I lost site of the land. I'm probably the only one on the boat who felt that way. I was determined, though, to be strong and courageous and tough it out. We finally made it to the other side and surprise, surprise, we didn't drown! I was rewarded with a fabulously beautiful beach to relax on.

Sometimes life feels like a violently rough boat ride as we are working to fulfill our purpose in life. Choppy. Uncertain. Scary. All we see is the wave. One trial after another. One uncertainty after another. Battle after battle. Yet, I will still dare to place my hope in Jesus.

God has a specific plan for each one of us. Be ready for whatever God has called you to do. You have no time to waste. It is always too soon to give up. God is our measure of success. Are we doing what He has asked us to do? Are we obedient? Is our motive pure? If so, then, we are successful. God's result expectation is different than man's. God's timing is His own. We need to do what we are supposed to do and He will manage the time.

> *"The greatest single cause of atheism in the world today is Christians who acknowledge Jesus with their lips. Then walk out the door and deny him by their lifestyle. That is what an unbelieving world simply finds unbelievable." — DC Talk*[xii]

When we fail to pursue God's plan for our life, we are essentially denying Him full access to our life. So, how do you know what God's plan is? What is your mission in life? What does God want you to do and be? What do you believe is important? What are you passionate about? Seriously think about these things. Here are a few tips for identifying your life mission.

- What are you passionate about? God creates each of us with personality and interests. I believe He allows us to be passionate about what He wants us to do.

As we pursue the Lord and develop an intimate relationship with Him, our desires and His desires align.

- What are your talents? If God has a plan for us (which He does), He will equip us to fulfill that plan. We have natural gifts and we have learned skills and abilities. When we do not have the natural gift or talent and we have yet to develop the skill or ability, we have to take some initiative and learn how to do what God calls us to do. However, a place to start is to see what skills, abilities, talents, gifts, and knowledge you have and how these match what you are passionate about.
- What is God saying to you? Listen as you pray and live life. Pay attention to the Word of God. Pray and seek God. Be still long enough to hear what He is saying to you. Whatever it is you sense God leading you to do, make sure it aligns with the Bible.
- What opportunities are available for you? This cannot be the first nor a stand-alone determination of God's plan. However, there are occasions when God does make opportunities available for us as a sign of what we are supposed to do. Make sure the opportunities align with God's word and other leading before you jump in.

Seriously think about God's plan for your life. Write it down as a mission statement. Your mission is fundamentally what you are about – your purpose in life. Your vision is what success in fulfilling your mission looks like. I love the definition of vision. Vision: "the ability to perceive something not actually visible, as through mental acuteness or keen foresight."[xiii] As you contemplate your mission and vision, don't allow thoughts of impossibilities to enter your mind. Remember, with God anything is possible.

Your Mission – What is your purpose in life? Look past who you are and what you are today. What did God create you to do?
Your Vision – What will success in fulfilling your mission look like?

Sometimes God's greatest opportunities for us mean taking a risk. Most of the time when we are completely committed to fulfilling what God has for us to do we will face trials and difficulties. It will not be an easy road. One of the best lessons I've learned in the past few years is to cognitively reprogram to live life like the answer God promised has already taken place. Cognitively reprogramming means adjusting our thought processes. If we adjust our thought processes to live like the answer has already happened, we are not overwhelmed by the difficulties we will face. We see the difficulties as stepping stones to reach what has already been accomplished. We don't live life blindly ignoring the stepping stones. We have to navigate each step, but we do it with the end in mind. In God's eyes, the answer has already taken place we just don't see it yet. Trusting Him means we hang on until we see what He has already seen.

We have to draw a line in the sand and not cross back over it. Choose to do what we know we're supposed to do and not what circumstances appear to dictate. It's really all about making a decision. The decision is to either tough out the storms and keep moving forward with God or do nothing and be consumed by circumstances or walk away and make your own way. I will do everything in God's power and with the attitudes of grace, love and compassion for others.

When Jimmy and I first started Clear Vision Ministries, we started really small and did what we could by personally funding the ministry. From 2003 to 2005 we began looking at other ways to generate funds so we could move things along a little better. We tried a lot of different strategies to raise money – each one requiring us to do some kind of work or investments but all still essentially coming from us personally. September 25, 2005, God spoke to Jimmy and told him we needed to be doing what we are supposed to do instead of working on other things to raise money. At this point, we consciously crossed over from being self-reliant to God-reliant for the funding. Sure we prayed God would provide before but we were trying to do it in our own power. We were truly relying on our own strength, intelligence and abilities. God wants us to rely on Him. Throughout 2005 God began speaking to me that it was almost time for me to quit my job. In January 2006, I knew I would be quitting by the end of the year. So, I began preparing for that and praying even more for God's provision. When I quit, there would be no income without God providing enough funding for CVM to operate and pay a salary. As we allowed God to be responsible for funding, we have been able to do more each year than the year before. Are we where we want to be? No. However, I know God is in control and He will ensure His plan is accomplished.

> *1 Thessalonians 5:24 He who calls you is faithful; He will surely do it.*

Part of the process of establishing a non-profit organization is approval by the IRS to allow the organization to accept charitable contributions and give tax-exempt credit for the donors. This is a hugely important process for fund-raising. We completed the paperwork ourselves in the fall of 2005. Jimmy and I spent about 100 hours completing the forms. We had experts tell us we would need an attorney to help us and we could expect to have a great deal of re-work on the application. We decided to let God take care of all those details. So, we completed the forms and sent them to IRS-land. We waited a year. Jimmy called the IRS several times to check on the status of our application. He was assured the form was received but they were about six months behind. (Okay, can you imagine being six months behind in your job and still being employed?) Each day as we checked the mail, we quickly flipped through the envelopes to see if we had an answer. On a sunny afternoon in October 2006, Jimmy was edging the yard. I went out to check the mail and was flipping through it as I walked back to the house. I saw an envelope from the IRS and immediately opened it. I sat the rest of the mail on the back of the car and ran out to Jimmy. The IRS had approved our 501(c)3 status. The scene was movie-like as we hugged and cried in the front yard. God had come through for us again. As we trust God, he will work out the details for us to fulfill His plan in our lives.

As we raise funds for CVM, we frequently have people tell us God is directing them to support us financially. More times than not, they do not follow through with the commitment. For a while, all of the commitment without follow-through was really hard for us. If we have to rely on people to support us to do what God has called us to do and they don't obey, then how can we fulfill God's plan for our lives. Then in His gentle way, the Lord smacked me on the back of the head and reminded me we are not relying on people to support us, we are relying on God to provide. Bam!

All I want – with every breath – is to go and do what God has placed in our hearts to do. Have you ever wanted something so bad you could smell it, taste it, see it, even when it wasn't right there with you? That is how I feel. I dream about being in Africa, China, Ecuador, Honduras,

Romania. I smell the smells. I feel the hands I hold. It is with me all the time.

For a few weeks at the end of 2008, Jimmy filled in for a small church in Kansas that was without a pastor. For lunch, the church would take us to the bowling alley to eat. Yes, the bowling alley. They had a Chinese/American buffet. Yes, the bowling alley. We left with a distinct smell in our clothes. Grease, smoke and I don't know what else. It was definitely unique. I could smell the bowling alley in my coat for weeks afterward. The smell stuck with us. A reminder of what we did, where we were and who we were with.

Before I had a chance to take my coat to the dry cleaner, we went to see my parents. They eat at a Mexican food restaurant several times a week. We ate there a few times during our visit. Now, my coat had an additional smell mixed in with the bowling alley smell. So, I had a Mexican food bowling alley smoky greasy smell following me wherever I went. Sounds lovely, huh!

Life is kind of like that. We come in contact with people and their scent rubs off on us. We go through things and it leaves a scent behind. We spend time with God and His scent settles on us. We become fragrant. A mixture of so many people and experiences lingers with us and follows us wherever we go. What does our scent say about us? As I sit here, I can smell Romania, Honduras, China, Ecuador, Jimmy, Taylor, Grandma's house, and the sweet fragrance of God. And I am moved at the core of my being.

Some things are etched in my mind in such a complete deep way. Pictures just can't tell the whole story. A picture doesn't have the smell, the feel, the complete story. I close my eyes and I see Inglies in Honduras, Anna in Fiji, Teacher Xu in China, Dimitru in Romania, the kids in San Cristobal. I feel the tears that have fallen from the cheeks of the people I've talked to and prayed with until their moistness turns into my own tears. I can see the look on the faces of our friends in Fiji when they saw their new church building. You can't capture it in a photo. I will never forget the breath-taking beauty of the Teleferico volcano in Quito, Ecuador. My heart aches every time I see in my memories the children in Romania playing in a field full of animal and human bones. These things stick with you for a lifetime. While I am captivated by the majesty of our great King, I also am overwhelmed by the great need in our world. Both of these emphatically compel me to action.

As we experience the process of fulfilling God's plan, we must keep our focus on Him. Hebrews 12:1-2 talks about keeping our eyes focused on Jesus. It is so easy to focus on circumstances or on trivial things and lose sight of Jesus. During our most difficult times of trial and testing, I saw myself losing focus numerous times. The key is to recognize we are losing focus and then refocus as soon as possible. I've worn glasses or contacts since the third grade. Every year since then my vision has changed. I can tell I need new contacts when I can't read signs when I'm driving or I find myself squinting a lot. I'm going to have some lovely wrinkles one of these days!! When I notice the blurry vision, I go see the eye doctor who helps me refocus my vision. Then, I can see clearly again.

While we were waiting to close on our house, I dreaded getting the mail because I knew there would be bills we couldn't pay. Then I looked in the refrigerator and we had no food. It was easy to focus on our need more than on Jesus. Some days, I lost my focus for a bit. Those were really lousy days. I had a choice where I placed my focus. When we do maintain a steady focus on Jesus, we make more progress in fulfilling His plan. It's like running a race. If you look around at the flowers, trees, people, stop to pick up a rock or get lost in the clouds, you will not win the race. In fact, you'll be lucky if you even finish the race. I have a hard time not walking into walls as it is. If I am looking around at other things, I can only imagine the disaster awaiting me!!

I see so many people floating through life without a real purpose. They may have a goal or something they want to accomplish but they are tossed around and easily distracted. I know what it's like to be temporarily distracted. However, I believe with everything within me we have to be intentional in how we live and in what we do. Is every moment of every day purposeful and productive? No. I wish it was. I don't want to waste a single breath. Look at your mission and vision. Now, think about the actions necessary to fulfill your mission. Create a list of action steps and use these action steps as a guide for living purposefully and productively.

Time is short and there's so much to do. Am I ready for heaven, for the rapture, for eternity with God – yes. But, there's so much to do. There are so many people who need to know Jesus. Every country we go to, my heart is torn because there are so many who live in darkness. I can't imagine how much greater the pain is for Jesus Christ who sacrificed for them.

In January 2007, I left my career to focus on Clear Vision Ministries. By this time, my health had made it impossible for me to work but my health didn't change what God has planned for us to do. The way we described it was "jumping out of the boat without a net." My job was our sole source of income. Jimmy had already been working full-time on the ministry but we were not able to take a salary. We really felt it was God's direction for us – and still do. This was the beginning of our season of miracles, faith and testing.

The entire summer and fall of 2007 was one battle after another, one problem after another. In October, I became seriously dizzy to the point I could not sit or stand without falling over. Even with several anti-dizzy pills, I still felt like I was going to fall out of bed at night. I saw a couple of specialists and was given a couple of different diagnosis, one which would require inner-cranial surgery and the other with no cure. This, of course, happened right before we were to leave for Romania. We were determined nothing was going to keep us from going on the trip, so we continued as planned. The moment I finished zipping our last suitcase to leave for Romania, the dizziness disappeared and has not returned!! Praise God!! I believe the key to the dizziness leaving was our obedience. Trust and obey always seem to go together when we are working to fulfill our purpose in life.

Habakkuk 1:5 Look among the nations, and see; wonder and be astounded. For I am doing a work in your days that you would not believe if told.

~ Sacrifice ~

While we were in Romania, we worked on the missionary's home, painted benches at a church, did children's outreaches, preached and conducted a children's worker training. After each trip, I ask Taylor to write a report on what he did, what he learned, etc. After Romania, he wrote: "When we went to the small villages, it made me feel that I am lucky to be living in America. Seeing the people there giving up so much of what little they had made me feel that people in America are not as close to God as they do not offer more of what they have even though it may be worth more but not compared to their everything." What are we willing to sacrifice to fulfill our mission in life?

I love the apostle Paul. I think he was probably a lot like me. He said what was on his mind and did it with conviction. As you read the words he penned in 2 Corinthians 4:8-13, you can sense his passion.

2 Corinthians 4:8 We are pressed on every side by troubles, but we are not crushed and broken. We are perplexed, but we don't give up and quit. 9 We are hunted down, but God never abandons us. We get knocked down, but we get up again and keep going. 10 Through suffering, these bodies of ours constantly share in the death of Jesus so that the life of Jesus may also be seen in our bodies. 11 Yes, we live under constant danger of death because we serve Jesus, so that the life of Jesus will be obvious in our dying bodies. 12 So we live in the face of death, but it has resulted in eternal life for you. 13 But we continue to preach because we have the same kind of faith the psalmist had when he said, "I believed in God, and so I speak."

I love the fact he was tough and persistent. Nothing stopped him from sharing the truth. The time when Paul and Silas were in prison (Acts 16) illustrates to me that we have a choice. They were in jail in chains. Instead of whining and complaining about the unfairness they were being subjected to, Paul and Silas chose to worship God. As they worshipped, the chains fell off and the doors opened. God set them free. We can choose to let the storms beat us down and prevent us from moving forward or we can choose to focus on God. They chose to focus on God and what happened? He rescued them and saved the jailer's family.

Have you ever noticed how quickly one negative thought or one minute of focus on visible circumstances can turn into an avalanche of despair? We adjust what we're looking at and it doesn't take long to become disoriented. I've been there too many times and I am always amazed at how quickly it happens. As we have been in the process of selling our house and trying to figure out what to do, I have been there. When I think about how much money we need to operate the ministry and how little we have, when I think about giving up our home, not knowing where we will live, if anywhere, I get lost in a swirling maze of thoughts that are not healthy. I get scared, confused and quickly do not even recognize myself. This probably sounds a little weird but I have looked at myself in the mirror and not even recognized myself. These moments are when we have to make a choice. I don't want to get lost in the circumstances, blown around like leaves in a storm.

Embrace the opportunities God gives you. Even when it looks scary, uncertain, bigger than you can handle, embrace it with the realization that God is the one who is going to do the work; you're just along for the ride. But, again, it is all reliant on your choice. Choice is a powerful thing.

My favorite poem is Robert Frost's The Road Not Taken. I think I like it so much because it fits with my life story. "The one less traveled by" offers adventure and a separation from the norm. The less traveled road is also a lot harder to walk down. One of the appealing aspects of the less traveled road is it is impossible to make the trip without an intensely intimate relationship with God. When you can't take a breath or move your foot forward without God holding you up, you will gain a new deeper understanding of who God is.

There comes a point in each of our lives, probably several times in life, where we have to decide if we are going to stay where we are or move forward with God. Moving forward will lead you down a less traveled road. This road can be terribly lonely. Logically, this makes sense. If it is less traveled, then, there are fewer people hanging out on the road. I think it is important to understand before you head down the less traveled road how some people will try to talk you out of it, most people will not understand what you're doing or why, some will walk away because it is too uncomfortable. It's important to know this so you're not blind-sided and discouraged along the way. I've been there. The intense sense of aloneness. The isolation. I've survived because Jesus is my constant companion. I've had days and nights where I have wept intensely, where I've felt like life was too much to bear any more, where I've felt so alone because no one got it – no one was in my space. Sometimes, I wondered if the tears would ever stop. But, God showed up. He was there all along but I recognized His presence with me as He wrapped His arms around me and let me cry on His shoulder.

A long time ago (in a land far far away), I had a dream. Actually, I had the dream the night Jimmy was called into the pastor's office in Louisiana. In this dream, I was walking through a marsh on planks. There would be a plank that seemed to be several feet long, but then all the sudden it would start to disappear. I would have to jump to the next plank. If I stood still, dark tentacles would come up out of the marsh and try to grab my feet. The only way to keep from being pulled under was to keep moving. As I traveled further into the marsh, I could see a light in the distance. If I kept my focus on the light, I could almost fly through the marsh. If we keep our focus on I AM, the journey down the less traveled road will be worth it – not necessarily easy, but worth it.

Every event leading me and Jimmy to where we are has been masterfully planned by God. Everything from the first job I had after we were married, which got me started in my career field, to the churches we worked at, to the friends we met in college have all in some way prepared us for the space we are in today. Even though the events in Louisiana were painful, they led us to the next ministry position. Two of the friends we met in college are now two of our board members. My first job in human resources started as a temporary position and I wasn't really even sure what I would be doing. I had no idea I would end up becoming a management consultant. I look at the people who are in my life right now and how they got there and I'm amazed. Get this – I found one of my friends in the phone book. I was the human resource manager for a company in Kansas at the time. In a management team meeting we decided we needed supervisor training for all levels of supervisors in the company. So, I started looking for a trainer. I flipped through the phone book and started making calls. The person we hired for the training project ended up being one of my closest friends. The phone call took place over ten years ago. Isn't it cool! God orchestrates events for all of our lives.

~ Run with Endurance ~

Run with endurance. This is a phrase I have heard repeatedly for the past couple of years but especially the last two months. You have probably heard the phrase or something similar (don't give up, be persistent, hang in there, tough it out, etc.). Most of my life when I've heard it, my thought was of course I'll endure. But, really I'm not sure I thought about it a whole lot. I'm learning running with endurance involves a tremendous amount of determination. It's not just a flippant effort. It is a concerted, intentional, fierce determination to not give up regardless of what comes. I sincerely believe as God calls us He expects us to run with endurance. If we let things stop us, we lose. We don't fulfill all He has for us to fulfill.

Run the race with endurance. Don't give up or give in even when obstacles get in the way. The walls surrounding you will crumble at the right time. Don't slow down. Keep running to the finish line and God will meet you there. I AM is with you throughout the race and is waiting for you at the finish line. Keep running – don't stop. People will try to pull you away and discourage you. Don't allow it. Keep your thoughts on Him. Keep your focus on Him. He will give you strength in battle. He will give you victory. It has already happened. You will see it in time. Victory is certain with God. He is never defeated.

Running with endurance is all about focusing on God and not on our circumstances. Focusing so intently that we are not distracted by anything no matter how intrusive the distractions are. Sometimes good things, pleasant things, seemingly harmless things can distract us from our purpose; from what it is God wants us to do. We get side-tracked. Next thing we know, we are on a different course and are further away from the 'finish line' instead of closer to it.

I'm not the most coordinated person in the world. I also can't draw a straight line to save my life, unless I have the aid of a ruler. Even then, I end up crooked sometimes. It's ok to laugh. I've laughed at the results many times. Without the ruler to keep me straight and some focal points along the way to make sure my straight line is going in the right direction, I end up in the wrong place. Life is similar. We need focal points in our life to make sure we're on track. We also need encouragers to make sure we are running with endurance, especially when we are facing storms in life.

I have several focal points. The best places to look to see if you're on track is the Bible and prayer. What is God saying? Jimmy is another great focal point and one of my biggest encouragers. I run things past him, ask him what he thinks and ask him what God is saying to him. I also have a couple of Confidant friends I can be completely open with and trust them to give me honest feedback. What are your focal points? Who are your encouragers? If you don't have any, I think it is a good idea to find some.

If there were no difficulties, we would not get to know God as our rescuer, our strength, our provision, our banner. I admit it is not fun to go through but it is amazing to see God work and to internalize who He is. As we prepared to go to China in 2008, it looked like the project was going to fall apart numerous times. It would have been so easy to just quit in March when we had to reschedule or when we didn't have the funding for the project or the people or when the airline prices were too high. We've had to remind ourselves often that we can't give up. We can't let circumstances dictate what we do. God is the one who is in control. He's the one who gives the directions. He's the one who makes all things possible. Even when all we see are impossibilities, if we continue with endurance, intense determination, God makes the impossible possible. Life is truly an adventure when you decide to endure. What we think of as just life is really our future in the making. Don't be surprised when God is faithful. It is His nature. In the end, I fully believe all of the delays and issues were in place to get us to China with the right people at the right time. Rest assured that God is putting everything in place for you at the right place and right time.

> *Psalm 33:11 But the LORD's plans stand firm forever; his intentions can never be shaken. (NLT)*

> *Jeremiah 29:11 For I know the plans I have for you," declares the Lord, "plans to prosper you and not to harm you, plans to give you hope and a future.*

> *Acts 13:22 I have found David the son of Jesse, a man after My heart, who will do all My will.*

Appendix – Application Questions

Chapter 1 – Pain is Such a Lonely Place

1) What pain are you currently experiencing?

2) What pain have you had in your past that still plagues you?

3) How are you surviving the loneliness associated with your pain? Who do you have to support you?

4) Is there someone you need to forgive for pain they have caused you? If so, it is time to forgive. Write down below who you need to forgive and why.

Now, ask God to help you forgive and say aloud the following:
__________________ (name of person) I forgive you for ________________________. What you did no longer has a hold on me. I will not revisit this again. I am moving on with God's help.

Chapter 2 – Spread it Out Before the Lord

1) Re-read Isaiah 40:28. What life circumstance are you facing right now that you need the everlasting God, Creator of the earth to help you through?

2) Now, it is time to spread it out before the Lord. Speak or write out your prayer pouring out your heart to God.

Chapter 3 – Messages From God

1) Have you ever felt like God is silent?

   yes

2) Do you have a place and time set aside to spend time with the Lord? If not, make a specific effort to spend time with the Lord regularly. If you have a hard time making time because of your schedule, put time on your calendar just as you would any other appointment.

yes, somtimes I don't get to it though

3) What has God been speaking to you?

4) What are some things in your life that remind you that God cares about you and your life?

Chapter 4 – Knowing God

1) Which of God's names stands out the most to you right now? Why?

2) What lessons has God been teaching you recently?

3) How have you applied what God is teaching you? If you haven't already applied the lesson, what do you need to do to apply what God is teaching you?

4) What can you praise God for? Start a list below.

Chapter 5 – Waiting Kind of Feels Like Being Lazy

1) What is most difficult about waiting for you?

2) What consequences have you faced in the past for acting too quickly, rather than waiting on the Lord?

3) Read Psalm 27. What are some things that stand out to you in this Psalm that give you hope?

4) How will you discipline yourself to wait on the Lord?

Chapter 6 – Relationships

1) Think about your friends. Who are your "Familiars", "Buddies", "Comrades", and "Confidants"?

2) If you do not have anyone in the "Comrades" or "Confidants" categories, look at the friends in your "Buddies" category to see if there are friends that you could invest more time and energy to develop the relationship further. Don't give up if you do not have friends in these categories yet. Pray and ask God to put the right people in your life.

3) Do you have unhealthy relationships that need to be salvaged or ended? If so, use the "I statement" model to communicate with your friend.

   When I (saw, heard, etc.)

   I felt (what emotion you felt)

   Because I (what interpretations support those feelings)

   Pause (let the other person respond)

   And now I would like (what action, information or commitment do you want now)

   So that (what positive results will that action lead to)

   What do you think? (listen to what the other person says – are they willing to do what is needed to make the relationship work or resolve the issue)

   For example: **When I heard** you say that I am about as close to being a genius as the rock in our front yard, **I felt** embarrassed and humiliated **because I** have worked hard to learn and improve my skills. (**pause**) **I would like** for you to not put me down or make fun of me **so that** I can talk to you without feeling hurt. **What do you think**?

4) Who is your accountability partner? If you do not have one, who could be your accountability partner? If you do not have regular interaction with your accountability partner, get out your calendar and schedule regular interaction. Use the questions in chapter 6 to guide your conversation with your accountability partner.

Chapter 7 – Finding My Voice

1) What are your values and priorities? What is most important to you? List your top five values/priorities.

    a.

    b.

    c.

    d.

    e.

2) What are you doing on a daily basis to support your top values and priorities?

3) What legacy do you want to leave behind?

4) What is most challenging to you in communicating with others? What steps will you take to work on these areas?

Chapter 8 – It's Okay to Rest

1) Is it difficult for you to rest? What did you learn from Elijah that you could apply to your life? (1 Kings 19:3-8)

2) Is your perspective skewed because of life circumstances? (Answer the questions in chapter 8.)

4) Rest. Do something today just for you.

Chapter 9 – So, Have You Ever Felt Like Habakkuk?

1) What is your view of God?

2) Where are you limiting Him in your life?

3) Will you choose to rejoice in the Lord as Habakkuk declares in Habakkuk 3:17-19?

Chapter 10 – Just Trust Me

1) What are your first thoughts when someone says "trust me"?

2) What are your thoughts when you hear the Lord say "trust me"?

3) List three reasons why you can trust the Lord.

   a.

   b.

   c.

4) What can you learn about God from the storm you are currently in?

Chapter 11 – Jesus, Please Make Me More Like You

1) Think about who Jesus is to you. Begin your own list of who He is below.

2) What do you need to change in your life to be more like Jesus?

3) What steps will you take to begin that change?

4) Talk to your accountability partner about the changes you need to make.

Chapter 12 – Fulfilling God's Plan

1) What has God asked you to do? Are you being obedient? Do you have pure motives?

2) What is your mission in life? Use the questions in chapter 12 to help you develop your personal mission and vision.

Your Mission – What is your purpose in life? Look past who you are and what you are today. What did God create you to do?
Your Vision – What will success in fulfilling your mission look like?

3) Where is your focus right now? Is it on God or on other things?

4) What are you willing to sacrifice to fulfill God's plan for your life?

References

[i] Pain. Dictionary.com. *Merriam-Webster's Medical Dictionary*. Merriam-Webster, Inc. http://dictionary.reference.com/browse/pain (accessed: March 15, 2009).

[ii] Henry, Matthew. "Commentary on Psalms 73". "Matthew Henry Complete Commentary on the Whole Bible". http://bible.crosswalk.com/Commentaries/MatthewHenryComplete/mhc-com.cgi?book=ps&chapter=073. 1706.

[iii] Audio Adrenaline. "Rest Easy." Don't Censor Me. ForeFront Records, 1993.

[iv] Fortner, Donald S., "The Names of God". http://www.freegrace.net/contents/framesnamesofgod.htm. (accessed: February 20, 2008).

[v] Smith, James. "Wait on the Lord." http://www.gracegems.org/SERMONS2/wait_on_the_lord.htm. (accessed: May 10, 2009).

[vi] Brown, Driver, Briggs and Gesenius. "Hebrew Lexicon entry for Qavah". "The KJV Old Testament Hebrew Lexicon". http://www.biblestudytools.net/Lexicons/Hebrew/heb.cgi?number=6960&version=kjv.

[vii] Kowalski, Peter B. (Director) (2009, April 20). I Would For You. Schwahn, M., Robbins, B., Prange, G., Tollin, M., Davola, J. (Executive Producers) *One Tree Hill.* Burbank, CA: Warner Bros.

[viii] Gill, John. "Commentary on Matthew 17:20". "John Gill's Exposition of the Bible". http://bible.crosswalk.com/Commentaries/GillsExpositionoftheBible/gil.cgi?book=mt&chapter=017&verse=020. 1999.

[ix] Exult. Dictionary.com. *Dictionary.com Unabridged (v1.1).* Random House, Inc. http://dictionary.reference.com/browse/exult (accessed: March 30, 2009).

[x] Alessandra, Tony and O'Connor, Michael J. 2006. *People Smart in Business.* New York: Morgan James Publishing. http://books.google.com/books?id=w6C-50_B9UUC&pg=PP3&dq=DISC+behavioral+style+description&source=gbs_selected_pages&cad=5#v=onepage&q=&f=false, (accessed June 1, 2009).

[xi] Trust. Dictionary.com. *Dictionary.com Unabridged (v 1.1).* Random House, Inc. http://dictionary2.classic.reference.com/browse/trust (accessed: May 05, 2009).

[xii] DC Talk. "What if I Stumble." Intermission: The Greatest Hits. ForeFront Records, 2000.

[xiii] Vision. Webster's New World College Dictionary. Your Dictionary. www.yourdictionary.com/vision (accessed: March 12, 2009).

LaVergne, TN USA
09 March 2010
175339LV00003B/1/P